With special t
Dr. S. Ad
and
Dr. Z. Anwar.

For my Friends and Family,
who stuck by my side through it all.
Dedicated to my Mum, Dad, Josh&Danielle who never gave up on me and loved me when I pushed them away. Daddy who held me, Mummy who never let me let go,
Danielle who treated me as normal human being and Josh who has been my rock loving me through the ups and downs.
As a reminder to Amelie that she is perfect in every way.

In the field where sunflowers grow.
Golden heads turn towards the sun, with shadows falling far behind.
Below the beating sun, amongst those golden heads, a little girl's face beams with joy.
Sunshine glows within her eyes and her face lights up with joy.
In the field where the sunflowers grow the little girl returns.
Each year.
Year after year the sun watches over the curly haired girl, a new photo captures her joy.
But then, In the field where the sunflowers grew the girl stands tired, emaciated and drained.
Eyes hollow, soul empty and her face no longer towards the sun, her soul no longer glows.
Instead she is consumed by the shadows of her mind.

In the fields where the sunflowers grow the girl returned, now a woman and once again she turns her face towards the sun.
She left her demons behind her in the shadows.
Sunshine lights up her eyes again and her face lights up with joy, a smile now shows that she is alive again.

## Prologue.

I have spent so long wondering how on earth I should start this book. Well, after 6 months of recovering YET again, here we go, it is time to tell my story. Currently I sit with my partner (Josh) and my two beautiful cats – PixieBelle and KasiaLily- in my own house and I figured now is as good a time as any to get started.

I have come a long way from the 17-year-old who decided to write a book, the cold and depressed girl who felt there was no meaning in her life. Perhaps my path would have been different should I have not faced the trials I did, but I would not re-write my journey and change my life for anything. It has taught me patience, strength, hope, faith and survival.

I have been to the depths of hell and back again, I have been given so many challenges in my life some for the good and some for the bad. I have been handed luck both good and bad and I have proven to myself that despite it all I am strong. I am privileged enough to have been able to help and support others and for that I am entirely grateful.

Ultimately, it is not the trials and tribulations you face, but how you choose to stand in the face of adversity and fight. I hope this book will educate not just family and friends but medical professionals too, through telling my own story and hopefully this will allow sufferers to see that there is a way out, you just have to be strong enough to look for it. I hope it shows you the ups and downs of recovery and provides you with reassurance that recovery is not linear, but it does not mean it is over.

My story did not quite work out the way I planned it but that does not mean it is not a story worth telling.

So, let's begin...

'I want to be like a Sunflower: so that even on the darkest days I will stand tall and find the sunlight'.
-Unknown

# Chapter One.
# The beginning.

I suppose I should give you a little bit of background first, right? Well, here we go ... 23 years ago, on a drizzly Friday evening at 10.30pm in the Leicester Royal Infirmary, a little girl was born, 6lbs 13oz, dark brown eyes and blonde hair glowing with a hint of fiery red.

I was quite small in length and in my features which Mum has always described as 'doll like' and she recalls looking down into my tiny eyes and telling me I was 'perfect'. 'Perfect' would be a phrase mentioned throughout my illness both for the good and bad: 'but you ARE perfect Chloe' (If only I could have believed that one!). From the moment I took my first breath I can honestly say felt loved, I was blessed. Oh, and if my parents only knew the journey this little baby would go on.

There was nothing, absolutely nothing to suggest what my future would hold. In fact, when this all came out Mum said if she thought it would happen to either of her daughters, she would have thought it would be Danielle (my elder and quieter sister). I was a fun-loving little girl, the life and soul of the party, the chatterbox and my parents were incredible in every way, I thrived. I hit every milestone on time -if not early- I was normal completely normal.

I was stubborn, in fact my stubbornness made me who I was and on one occasion Dad returned home to me standing at the top of the stairs and Mum at the bottom, -both of us arms crossed and stern faces, 'how long have you been like this?' he asked before Mum responded in a stern voice 'half an hour and I WILL get her to come down'. Unfortunately, my independence and stubbornness would be both a blessing and a curse throughout my time with my disorder.

I was and would always remain eager to please people and to be the very best, at my two year check my mum recalls answering the Dr's question's 'can she draw circles?' he asked, 'I don't think she can 'she replied, well I did! In fact, it was a perfect one as well -of course, what else would be acceptable?!-, I pointed to the crayon stating 'yellow' and my mum once again responded 'everything is Yellow at the moment. It's her favourite colour.' My Dr once again tests me 'what colour is this one?' ..... 'blue', right again. The only thing I fell behind in was my weight (kind of ironic when you think about it!).

As a little girl I always loved yellow, I grew up talking of my favourite colour being Yellow simply because... it 'made people smile'. Throughout my entire life that is something I have cherished: peoples smiles, peoples happiness. I loved how the sun shone, making all the colours below even brighter, brightening everyone's smile. I loved how sunflowers followed the sun (There were many years of photos by sunflowers in France) and they knew to leave their darkness behind them, I LOVED yellow. Correction...Love.

Everything I wore from the age that I could choose until I was about 12 was yellow, it suddenly became 'uncool' and I was foolish enough to follow the crowd. My soul is splashed in Yellow, my heart beats for all it stands for, the fire in my heart and spirit, my ability to make people smile and my joy when I make peoples day, I embody all that yellow stands for.

I grew up loving life, people and animals with my entire being. I was known for giving a glowing and bubbly smile to everyone passing by; peoples happiness meant the world to me. I wore my heart on my sleeve always (this would become a problem over the years) and I suppose if you were to ask the people around me as I grew up who I was, I would probably be described as the little girl who always had something to say. The sassy energized little girl dressed in every shade of yellow, curls spiralling around my face and always wearing a big cheeky smile. I cared about everyone, handing out hugs with my big brown eyes sparkling with excitement always. I laughed and performed, I loved being centre stage and I loved making people happy.

Growing up we would build castles out of cardboard boxes, mega blox towers surrounding our poor cat, pick leaves off the floor in the autumn and create patterns, collages and paintings with them. My childhood was picturesque from year to year and my Imagination and creative sense would blossom throughout the years.

Throughout my childhood, we would have many amazing holidays and adventures abroad and every time we went to France I would practically live in the pool, always called a 'water baby'. Diving to the pool floor and swimming on my back, pretending to be a mermaid just like Ariel with my auburn curls flowing.

Somehow, I would manage to acquire a stream of free gifts from shop owners and market sellers, they would smile and hand me things over and over! I HAD to be the one speaking French (overachiever here!) and I HAD to stop at every field to stand beside yet another sunflower, face beaming as the camera would capture yet another year of holidays. I loved spending time just us four, playing in the pools, exploring new places and foods. France was our almost yearly holiday, consisting of Chateau visits, vineyard tours and bike rides.

I cared about everyone: I was brimming with questions, my vocabulary exceeding many children my age with my favourite at this age being 'fortunately' (not to be a brag here). I would perform to an audience of teddy bears, dolls and quite often unwilling family members singing at the top of my lung's songs like 'reach' by S Club 7, Abba and when the time came of course... my hero Demi Lovato. I loved music, it embedded itself in my heart at an early age... I was boisterous and had no fear of food (I mean apart from Brussel sprouts!), I was as my mum would always say 'the easier one' when it came to food.

At 4 years old I began to attend dance class, I attempted one lesson of ballet and ran back to mum halfway through, hands on hips and pouting 'I can't do it Mummy it's too floaty'. Alas, tap dancing went down a treat, with stomping feet and clipping heels I danced my little feet off. I can still recall my first show, we did an Annie dance, and I took the role very seriously. I loved Modern and Acro as well, I got such a buzz from performing: the blue eyeshadow and red lips standing in front of an audience. I began to put shows on in our living room and at all of our family parties (looking back I feel VERY sorry for them all!), I would play my clarinet (which I hated), dance, sing and act.

When the days of leaf collages, baking with Grandma or painting with Gran passed by it was time to start primary school. I think it was.an easier transition than many of my peers, mainly because of my big sister Danielle, she was and still is my best friend. I did however run out every single day, straight into my Mums arms, where I would babble on about all of the drama of my day before being sent back for something I forgot, Miss Barnes always standing in the classroom pointing to where I'd left it.

I do not quite know how to explain how that light inside of me, that bright light that glowed from my soul suddenly turned from yellow to black. How the fire burnt out leaving only darkness behind or how suddenly that smile became all too distant, a mere memory to those around me. The curls first became straightened to conform to what I was told was beauty and then as my brain began to be engulfed by my Anorexia it fell out, eventually that bubbly girl became a hollow shell of who she once was.

I was 7 years old when my happiness began to bleed out of me, I was bullied and tormented, my need to please people became my demise and before I knew it, I had met Ana. Ana would be later known medically as Anorexia Nervosa, of course I had no idea what it was when I was that young and I was always told that I had an imagination so I just assumed other people had this voice too.

Ana was manipulative and clever, oh so clever, she had a way of making me feel both safe and scared, she was able to turn me against everyone, convince me of things that were not real. Ana slowly took everything from me: friends, family and my soul.

I belonged to Anorexia, she had her friends of course because no one has a prisoner of war without the required guards to keep the prisoner's spirits down, tire them out and break them. There was Anxiety, Depression, Self-Harm, Self-loathing, body dysmorphia and of course a bundle of mismatched jumbled emotions to which no one knew the name for... yet.

There is something in the way that Anorexia Nervosa works, trapping the victim in a web of lies, inescapable guilt and self-hate. Breaking all the connections you have with those around you, isolating you and pulling you further into the abyss. Anorexia promised me the sun the moon and the stars; she promised she would make everything better if I just listened and followed her rules.... She was my best friend, or so I thought. Whilst the girls who bullied me and the rest of my class were playing at lunch, I was counting calories, hiding food and over exercising. My sister's future mother-in-law happened to notice me going to bin my sandwiches and so sent me right back to eat. I guess at the time it just looked like a little girl eager to go and play but she got me back on track after that. Albeit I was Indulging in occasional self-harm behaviours such as biting, hair pulling and punching. Eventually the child inside of me wanted to play and decided the reason she could not was because she was too tired because she was not eating enough.

It is crazy isn't it? That a seven year old can see that food is what she needed to keep up with her peers and be happy and yet for the next 16 years despite seeming to the world to be a normal girl , she wouldn't be able to see that. Ana stayed in my mind and slowly piece by piece she consumed me and all that I was became a memory.

Anorexia works as a numbing agent to its victims, distracting them from the pain of uncertainty of their own lives, providing them with a sense of control and isolating them into one obsessive coping mechanism. Essentially that is why it is classed as an addiction, as much as an alcoholic would reach for a bottle or a heroin addict would seek out the drug. There is something in my brain, something that encourages and craves this constant need to be better, to be perfect, to be empty and this is where Anorexia caught me.

Watching the number go lower and lower and knowing that I was finally good at something only pulled me further into my disorder. I was good at this I thought, I may not be like the other girls, I may be stupid and not important but I could do this, I could lose weight faster than I had ever imagined and this fed my desire to be perfect and to be liked. I suppose if you asked everyone around me, they would argue there was many things I was good at and so many things that made me ... ME but I just couldn't and still struggle to accept that.

How did I become vulnerable to my disorder ? well you see I think some of us are born with the disorder it just takes certain events to wake it up and bring it to the surface. For me, I remember the moment she first arrived, I had been in the girls bathroom and a group of girls who had been bullying me had just left, I was in tears and I remember looking into the mirror with pure hatred of what stared back at me. Then, I heard her "They're right, you have to be pretty or thin to be liked and you'll never be pretty, so you have to be thin." And so, it began. I wish I could go back and tell that little girl the dangers of trusting this demon. It is important to note at this point however that Anorexia is not vanity it is a serious disorder, and it feeds off of insecurities and a feeling of being out of control of the stressors in life and through these it gains initial control.

I think I always had issues with my self-esteem, always wanted to be someone else to fit in but this is what made me vulnerable to Ana. Each morning I woke with the same voice shouting at me; " Don't eat that, why are you eating you're so fat, I'm only trying to help, everyone is laughing at how fat and ugly you are. Look at how vile you are, stop eating, you don't deserve food or love, you might as well die because you'll never be thin enough or pretty enough". I began making myself sick after dinner and even after water or small snack although this only lasted a month or so. Many believe Purging is Bulimia however Bulimia is categorized by consuming an unusual amounts of calories in one sitting and purging whereas many Anorexics engage in the behaviour just without the binge.

Growing up, I had the best childhood, and this follows me. I remember being that carefree little girl, running around our garden, walking up to my Grandmas for family lunches, painting and sketching with Gran and going out and about always experiencing new things. My imagination being for the good not for the bad, tossing leaves up in the air like Sandra Bullock in practical magic, telling myself I would only ever fall in love if he had 'bluey green eyes'. I loved magic and make believe. What bothers me most about these illnesses is that often people (especially medical professionals) try and pin it down to parents, this was the case throughout the majority of my CAMHS (Child and Adolescent Mental Health Service) journey but I digress...to me my childhood was perfect.

## A mother's point of view:

Well as Chloe has said, she arrived, very quickly, on 4$^{th}$ April 1997. She made our family complete. Loved her from the start. Danielle had someone to play with and argue with too! There were arguments as any family had. That was normal. We were all normal!

What really annoys me about this awful disease is that they try to find a reason for it to have developed. Always looking into her past. Always trying to find a pivotal point for when it engulfed her life and took over our whole family. There wasn't one. Simple.

We have since found that they are born with it. This has filled me with guilt since, as I feel I must have done something wrong to create such an evil monster inside my daughter's head. Yes, she was bullied. I was too. So, I was keen and quick to get it sorted asap. Even sending her to a different high school with new friends to start over.

Unfortunately, Ana had already consumed Chloe and we were still ignorant to the whole thing. To this day, I wish she had just told us, explained what was happening in her head. But would I have believed her? We knew nothing about mental illness, nothing about eating disorders, perhaps we would have told her to snap out of it. A phrase I used to start with, that has become something that people always said to me.... try saying that, they would say.... Oh wow... never thought of that. Really? If I could put the emoji of the woman slapping her face on the page now I would!

As the years progressed, we watched Chloe disappear in front of our eyes. I remember her telling me she had Anorexia for the first time, she had been told by the school nurse to tell me or they would. I was totally shocked and confused. You eat, I said.... she played it down majorly, obviously the voice directing her in what to say. So, we continued to be oblivious for a while and then our trips to CAMHS started. More of my experience with them later.

Chloe went from this carefree little bubbly girl, to a withdrawn, no confidence and moody girl within weeks. It was putting immense pressure on our family and we were sinking

'Don't judge me. You know my name but NOT my story'.
- Demi Lovato.

# Chapter Two.
## Paving the way for Anorexia.

I left my primary school a year early like my sister had done, she too had been bullied so both of us moved to Abington high school instead of Saint Pauls Catholic high school. Neither of us cared too much about leaving early, I think the final straw was when my teacher told my parents at parents evening that 'catholic children just don't bully'.

When I moved to Abington I made friends reasonably fast, I remember becoming very close to Megan whom I really enjoyed spending time with, but as the term went on I guess my popularity just didn't match hers and I was left behind. Luckily, I found further friendship in Emily, Rosie and Alanis. I got through my high school years loving Drama, acing food technology (yeah, I will blow my own trumpet there), gossiping and yes this did land me and Rosie in trouble a fair bit. I performed in the year 6 talent show which Mum was so proud of as I had only been at the school for a few months.

My sister's year group (who sat in the balcony) were cheering and singing along although- I am not sure if that was because of her popularity, their genuine encouragement or them making fun of me. My brain selected the latter.

My lungs began to turn on me in year 7 and I spent a lot of time in and out of the HDU (High dependency unit) in hospital due to my Asthma. This left me with a lot of time with my own brain which allowed me to become more and more self-critical, at the time there were already so many things I was insecure about, the boys in BI (a form group next door to mine) would call me 'brick chewer' because my teeth were wonky. Anyway… back to my dull hospital bed and crappy lungs! Constant Asthma attacks meant I could no longer sprint as well anymore which was something, I was actually good at (as well as hurdles) and my constant stream of steroids lead to weight gain and bloating which you can imagine did not go down very well.

I cringe looking back at myself in any photos at this time and they truly haunt me which breaks my Mums heart I know. I would begin to pinch and pull at the lumps of fat, weighing up how much each handful weighed and how much I needed to use. I saw myself at the back of the dance shows being a confirmation of my failures and unattractiveness. My best friend Laura seemed effortlessly flawless and she had her own friendship group at dancing leaving me with mine (one of whom poked fun of me as my disorder worsened, thanks for that).

Alongside this, my sister became sick and this led me to worry constantly. I did not know how to make her better and I missed her so much. My loneliness and Anxiety grew, and I remember having to see a councillor at High school when it all got too much following my Dads hernia operation (Christmas). Now I know this seems very overdramatic (yes here we go with my 'drama queen' digs) but I really was drowning in emotions, self-hate and paranoia. I was praying for my period so that I would fit in but did not put it together that skipping meals was not helping, I wanted to fit in and I wanted control over my emotions, so I began to lie, I used my lunch money to buy my friends food: 'perfect' I would think to myself, 'I'm not wasting money by buying things and binning them and I am making my friends happy'.

Makeup became my mask and my straighteners my armour, each day I would fry those curls straight and cover my skin in foundation (I actually had really nice skin, I always have so I'm not entirely sure why I was applying so much). I always wanted my sister's approval and I wanted to be with her all the time which really pushed her further away as her annoyance towards her baby sister grew. At one point we were arguing and somehow, I managed to get her detention for bullying which to this day I find both funny and feel awful for at the same time! Sorry D!!!

Danielle left Abington and moved to college when I was in year 7 and suddenly, I had to figure things out for myself. I worked hard to get high marks (I did just that except in Maths) but Maths was my biggest fear and remains my fear, why? Because I cannot do it, it makes me feel stupid and this does not bode well with my perfectionism. Thus, I give up because I can't be 'perfect' at it and I get embarrassed, with Miss Hefford our new teacher came a sudden change in my Maths and before I knew it, I was moved up a set. This did not end well however and I stood answering a question after being put on the spot as a punishment for talking (I was just asking Emily for help!). 'You're an idiot, the whole class is looking at you, can't you see them laughing? You're a failure', tears streamed down my face and I hung my head in shame. Mr Anthony sent me out of the class to calm down and came out to apologise, he later became one of my favourite teachers and would get me to understand, achieving really good marks finally ( just in time to move to college).

In that same year I had boy issues (obviously) and remember my boyfriend breaking up with me for one of the 'populars' using 'that's the way the cookie crumbles' I mean, seriously? I really wish I had laughed back then instead of being upset because really who uses a line from a film to break up! I also remember my ex Max and some other guy that I cannot remember! Throwing a dictionary at my head calling me something like a 'nerd' or the equivalent, again tearing down my self-esteem and my embarrassment grew.

By the time college came around I was pretty beaten down by my high school bullies and the girl on the corner of my road who would bully me on my walk home. I arrived at Guthlaxton college breathing a sigh of relief that I had new classes and was finally around my big sister again (at this point she was healthy again, apart from laryngitis on and off!). I was lucky because she made such a good impression on everyone, she met that it paved the way for schoolteachers to warm to me. By this point I was exercising more and skipping meals, slicing my wrists whenever I felt that pit of self-hate grow. My friendship group grew, and I found friends who were genuine, I adored my Drama lessons and would have such a laugh with Eilish, Chloe and Amy. I would talk all things Demi Lovato in science with Abby and in form time with Beth and Jess, there were a few snide remarks from boys here and there making me feel worthless and stupid, but my friendships made it easier.

I think my Anorexia was definitely fuelled by my perfectionism but I always felt like I had to try so hard to fit in and to get people to like me and I really do wish I could go back and tell myself that you can't make everyone like you. It is almost impossible to have everyone like you, I always came across as so independent and self-confident but really, I felt so different. Have you ever been in a crowded room, people talking and laughing yet you are utterly alone? Well that is how I felt and perhaps still feel. I felt/feel unworthy of people affections, I was always wondering if people truly did like me or if it was all a pity fest. The smiles, hugs and 'lovely to see you' remarks for me always had a hidden meaning in my mind which was more often than not 'ugh I wish I didn't have to talk to you'.

Anorexia saw and exploited my weaknesses and knowing that makes me furious! I see a dark demon reaching out to a seven year old me , pulling me in for a hug, telling me she loves me and that I am safe before quickly grasping me with her claws and dragging the real me back to the depths of my brain.

I had a bad experience with a 'boyfriend' (different school and older) in year 11 and unfortunately his hard hit made me feel like I had disappointed him ( I wouldn't have sex with him) yet my red-headed temper saw me fight myself free and leave him. That's not to say that he didn't then constantly message me on BM (Yes when that existed, I know I'm aging) and yes I was gullible enough to believe him and if it wasn't for Wednesday and Sophie I probably would've gone back to him.

I'm a bit of a walk over or at least I used to be , Mum always told me I didn't have to be the first to apologise with friends especially when it wasn't my fault but I was also easy to forgive. One of the other stressors in my life at this point was my big sisters health, I was so worried about her and despite a family member thinking I was doing what I was doing for attention (ah yes that old belief) I was genuinely just worried about her and that meant I relied a little more on controlling the whirlwind of emotions inside me . I then lost it with a childhood friend when she decided to flip out at dancing when I told her she had gone wrong, she told me that me and my sister 'enjoyed' being sick... idiot.

I was having regular asthma attacks at this point and my lip was going through a phase of swelling randomly of which me and my best friend referred to as my 'duck lips'. Understandably this did NOT help my self-esteem, neither did the day at college where we had some NHS 'healthy living' thing in which I was told a BMI of 19 was Fat... I'll just leave that there.

## A mother's point of view:

School is tough, I remember when I was at school, all I wanted to do was to leave! I hated it. People say, school is the best part of your lives, enjoy it. I say, no way. So, I suppose, Chloe's experience was similar to mine, only with a mental illness in tow too.

I will say, everyone that knew Chloe, loved Chloe. It is a real shame, that even now at 23 she still does not believe this. People say daft and silly things and whereas you and I brush them off, Chloe takes it to heart. This is not a bad thing, but it makes her vulnerable to the bullies of this world.

Wednesday was truly and still is a loyal beautiful girl, who if she had not been on the scene, I dread to think how this would have turned out. For this I will always be grateful. One good thing that can come from school-life, is finding a friend for life.

Thankfully, Chloe found hers here. Her sister was poorly for a few years, I suppose this led to us not noticing Chloe's demise into the depths of anorexia. I can continue to beat myself up over what I missed or brushed off, or I can give myself the benefit of the doubt and say, we are only human. I will say, once I knew what was happening...... boy was I on it!

'The pride in continuing your journey is far greater than the comfort of retreating'.

# Chapter Three.
## The girl to the right and the appointment from hell.

Induction week, it only seems right that this friendship gets its own chapter so here we go. I had had an awful lesson before and felt horrendous about myself, my voice was stupid, I tried too hard and no one liked me and even if they did it was out of pity, right?

I slumped onto my backless art stool (I hate those stools) next to the girl who honestly scared me, she was from South Wigston High School and was the complete opposite to me. In all honesty she made me terrified, I smiled and sat beside her and to my surprise she smiled at me. 'Phew' I thought to myself and then it happened ... 'Wednesday' the teacher called out 'No Miss it's Tuesday' I replied, she repeated and I turned to the girl who had smiled at me stating 'as if someone would be called Wednesday, how stupid'. She raised her hand 'Yes Miss', I died of complete embarrassment and spent half the lesson facing away mortified by what I had done and utterly terrified that she was going to punch me as soon as the lesson was over. Alas, this led to me drawing with my left hand (not my best work) and avoiding any eye contact at all.

This oddly named girl would become my best friend, my sister and my hero. She would become the Christina Yang to my Meredith Grey, and she would also become Anorexia's enemy.

I am so thankful for this friendship because it honestly made college a good time for me despite all of the other stuff going on in my life. Most of my years in school had been plagued by bullies, 'popular' girls who totted around looking down their noses at everyone else or beating myself up about my failures. Instead me and Wednesday would spend our lunches and breaks in art or in Wendy's (the college restaurant) and despite our differences we were inseparable to the point that eventually she would just refer to my Mum as 'Momma'. Daddy would often joke she was part of the furniture and yes in true Dad style he would call her Tuesday!!

Wednesday noticed something was off in year 11, suddenly I began stopping my lunch (salad), I became withdrawn and my arms became covered in bracelets. Somehow I managed to keep a few people at bay, I would go to the toilet in lessons, doing a lap around the school before returning, my legs would jiggle about under the desk and Coke Zero became a constant desk feature.

Abby noticed my wrists following an asthma attack as we sat together in the medical room, she pressed me for answers and it finally came out. We just sat together in silence listening to Demi Lovato on my phone when I swore her to secrecy but somehow, she managed to convince me to let her tell Wednesday. I remember seeing Abby stop her on the stairs, I froze as I saw Wednesdays face drop. The thing is, me and Eddy (her nickname) were inseparable, and we were/are like sisters so when I saw her face drop, I knew instantly shit was about to hit the fan (excuse my language).

I walked so fast into the courtyard hoping that she would not face me there, but she grabbed my arm pulling me to one side and demanding to see my wrists, demanding I took off my jumper. I never saw her speechless and the look of fear in her eyes made my blood curdle and then it happened "I'm worried about you Chlolo"... how dare she Ana screamed, I was mortified could she not see I was still so fat, I was fooling myself as my clothes hung looser around my shrinking frame.

This all unfolded after a New year where I had had too much to drink and blurted it out to a family friend, looking back I still regret not going to my big sister, I honestly believe she would've come up with a plan and kept my secret until necessary but alas my Mum was told and we got into a huge fight (NYE was never the same after that, at least for a good 5 years). I cannot apologise enough for that, I lied to Mum telling her it was over, and I was not doing that anymore, that I was just having a rough patch. She supervised me for a few weeks, but my manipulation meant I still got away with it.

I ended up being convinced to see the school nurse whom I instantly recognised, she had come into my primary school years ago and drilled it into us that chocolate, sweets and red meat were all 'bad' she actually got my sister scared of chocolate for a while (Mum went bonkers... understandably). As a result, we were already off to a bad start, I sat in silence for most of the appointment and then she said it 'stand on the scales' hatred grew inside me and I was furious to be put in this position, I glared at my friend who bless her was such a good friend back then and I felt like any chance of help was over. She proceeded to tell me that I had an 'eating disorder'. Not a chance I thought, I did not binge, and I rarely made myself sick, only if I swallowed chewing gum or cucumber by accident because of the extra calories. I still ate dinner or at least some of it so there was no chance I had an eating disorder "TOO FAT" the voice screamed, this nurse told me she was referring me to **CAMHS** before proceeding to tell me that I had a day to tell my Mum else she would.

I was utterly seething that she would dare put me in this position, I was still so fat, why did I ever say anything?! Why had I agreed to go to this meeting? how could I pacify these people and stop them from suffocating me and destroying my work?!

I wrote Mum a letter and when she was in her room I followed her in "I need to talk to you, I don't want you to talk until I finish" I said with my voice crackling in fear as I sat on her bed. I cannot remember exactly what the letter said but I remember her response sealing my beliefs and proving Anorexia right, I felt like a fool and a fake. "What do you mean an eating disorder?" she said with a red face and anger brewing "you eat, you don't have an eating disorder, you just need to do it healthily, we will do it together". Needless to say, this didn't last for long. Wednesday stuck by my side throughout, listening to my rants and trying to convince me to eat, my lunch often ended up straight in the bin as Mum had begun to pack me salads etc (simply putting it down to a phase).

## A mother's point of view:

'My nightmare started in January 2014, Chloe had been suffering from Anorexia since she was seven, this was the first I heard of it. She looked ok, didn't she? Yes, she has lost weight, but she has been watching what she eats. She was using her reserves, water loading before weigh ins and now my baby girl was self-harming and torturing her body.'

## A best friend's point of view:

When we first met, I could not help but find some humour in the fact that she had no idea that Wednesday was my actual name. Karma as she sat drawing with the other hand (terribly I have to say). She seemed like a nice person and so It was no surprise that we became inseparable. When Abby told me, what was going on it only confirmed my suspicions, and I was crushed and as much as I wanted to tell Helen (her mum) I was so worried about how Chloe would react and what she would/could do if I did.

See, her Anorexia makes her do some stupid stuff and I had to protect her from that even though it meant keeping her secret. I was lucky that she did listen to me to an extent.

'Even if something seems like it can't be fixed, doesn't mean it's broken'
- April Kepner, Grey's Anatomy.

# Chapter Four
## CAMHS, the French teacher and the music tour.

Ah, CAMHS... where to begin on the joyous and helpful experience (NOT). Walking down the path to Oakham house I was terrified, at this point Mum still did not really see too much of an issue nor did she or anyone in our family know anything about eating disorders. I guess because I was not the media image of Anorexia at the time, she was not too concerned. I remember walking in with my sister by my side which gave me a sense of relief and security, but I was completely unsure of what to expect. I vividly remember sitting across from a girl who was the media representation (I really hope she made it), she had a beanie on and I remember thinking in a sick way ' I wish I was that thin', I'm not proud of that thought and it amazes me how sick the thought process of this evil disease is.

She had a bald patch under her hat when she took it off to adjust it and her skin was covered in lanugo, it's strange to think that in a surreal way, I was staring at my future self. A blonde lady walked out (Nicky I think her name was) and called out 'Miss Chloe Shelton please', my sister gave me an encouraging smile and whipped her phone out to tell Mummy that I had gone in. I remember answering all the questions they asked and wondering how on earth my birth could impact this illness. I would have to wait for a few weeks before I had a diagnosis, the letter came through stating that because my **BMI** was not below 18.5 I would be going to a different centre for 'depression'... yes, that's right they completely dismissed my Anorexia.

Ana then used this as ammunition 'see you don't deserve help, you aren't thin enough', the disorder would progress rapidly, spiralling faster and faster. Natasha was the name of my CAMHS worker I believe, and she spent pretty much every session trying to find a textbook cause of my Anorexia and using the same phrase over and over 'how does that make you feel?'. Meanwhile I had discovered I could mask my weight by hiding things in my bra and tying coins into a bun in my hair. The scales showed a lower number each time but at least I had that cover, right? Wrong. There's only so far that inanimate objects can get you and the weight was too obviously dropping.

Mrs Turner was one person who could see where this was heading way before most (this lady is amazing). Turner was my French teacher and we got on straight away, I owe Danielle a lot as her first impression on people became a solid starting point for me and everyone likes my sister. Turner and I can both remember one memory vividly, we had just been on break and whilst walking back into college she exclaimed 'Shelton' and took a sharp breath in before telling me I was looking too thin and to be careful. Mrs Hadkiss was next to notice (my P.E. teacher), probably because my P.E. t-shirt was miles too big on me suddenly and when she began to question it her beliefs were quickly confirmed as I conveniently felt unwell in our theory lesson about eating disorders. In all honesty the class staring at me as I squirmed in my seat tells me that they more than likely knew. I remember Turner spotted some marks on my knuckles once when I was purging if I swallowed gum by accident (yep, gum) and called me out on that.

Binging is never something I have engaged in and I always make that clear, self-induced vomiting is not always Bulimia and it does not always follow a binge. In my case however momentary I would make myself sick should I have swallowed chewing gum or cucumber.

Summer came around and we went on music tour. Music tour was an event in which the college big band, concert band and choir would all go away and perform abroad, I was in concert band and choir and had forced Wednesday into choir that year so she could come on tour! Mum felt reassured when she found out Turner was coming, and James (Danielle's friend) would be there too, she updated Mrs Turner and she assured Mum she would keep an eye out and boy did she do just that .

Turner had watched me on the ferry and although I was not eating, she did not think I was too bad, but I guess that changed fast when she had to spend a week with me. When we arrived at our hotel Wednesday, me and the other two girls settled in. In retrospect, this room was the worst possible environment with 3 out of 4 of us self-harming regularly! What was ironic was that our room had no lock on the bathroom! Anyway, we settled in and Wednesday snuck out to tell Turner that I hadn't eaten in over 24 hours (she knew Turner had a way around me), she came straight in and finally got me eating a few pieces of fruit.

Turner would have to face Anorexia a fair few times that holiday, one involved Wednesday and her tricking me into sitting by the window on the coach whilst Wednesday switched places and left me wedged by the window with Mrs Turner blocking me from escape holding a bag of Lays ready salted crisps that she insisted I ate (this was back when I would try and please people if I could). I also spent the second half of the week sitting at the teachers table with Wednesday so that Mrs Turner could monitor me.

When we got home I immediately went on holiday with my Family to Lanzarote (one of my favourite places in the world) I ate well and had the most amazing salad (I still dream about this salad... it was unbelievable) I was still trying to please my family and pretend I was ok at this point and Ana wanted them to believe I was ok and I hadn't developed any tricks at this point. We found a bar that we went to regularly and met Nikki who became such a positive influence in my life, she made me smile so much on that holiday. Dean (my brother-in-law) had me in hysterics most of the time, we always got on so well and I cannot apologise enough for letting him down, he has always been my big brother and I have so many memories from that holiday of playing pool and winding each other (and Danielle) up. I remember cackling away with tears streaming down my face as he sat on the other side of our camel ride pulling his 'what the hell have I agreed to' face. What I hate was that I was just about to hit rock bottom, I remember hugging Nikki goodbye and feeling this sense of fear as we boarded the plane and like the time before, staring out of the window tears pooled in my eyes as I left my happy place.

The next holiday we would have would be so very different for us all. I remember being weighed at the valentine's centre and thinking I must have gained loads, but I had not, I had lost! I guess France had set me up for room to gain some having lost so much then and then Lanzarote had fed me up, but the walking and swimming must have burnt it all off.

When we got home we spent some time with family and friends and I remember having the most carefree time messing about with my childhood best friends Joe and Laura at Bradgate park with Anita and Grace, Mum and Danielle and it truly was a time where I felt in control, I felt like I was in control of my restricting and that if I wanted to I could stop... I was so very wrong.

## A mother's point of view:

Camhs....... the most hateful place in the world. the place where I put all my trust and hope, only for them to let us down when we needed them the most. But more to come on my relationship with this place later!

Why did you let her go on music tour? I hear you yell.... why did you take her on holiday? These are questions I have been asked many a time. Every time I replied, we were trying to keep Chloe busy, remind her she was loved. Remind her she had a life worth fighting for. I honestly believe this worked; I stand by my judgements.

I'm not sure if you can tell or not yet, I have a stubbornness in me, that thankfully both my girls have inherited from me. My determination to carry things out, to get answers and to remain strong has always been a big part of my being. I started to see that Chloe would listen and we could come to a compromise about food, exercise and drinking. this would change as the illness took over, but the anorexia really DIDN'T LIKE ME!!!

## A best friend's point of view:

France showed me how bad things were getting and although we had a really good time, Anorexia did plague the trip. Ana had her claws in from the start and that was evident. I knew Turner would be able to get through to her to an extent and so I went to her, she was almost a school mum, so it was easy to confide in her.

I told her Chlo had not eaten since the night before we left so over 24hours and she came straight to our room and refused to leave until she had eaten some fruit. It dawned on me that I would be face to face with Ana a lot this trip as Chlo's dead eyes glared at me. I ended up losing my temper a few days in and sitting on her to force feed her after she threw an apple out the window refusing it, I held her down and tried to get her to eat ... she bit me and pulled at my hair, it was like a cornered animal attacking.

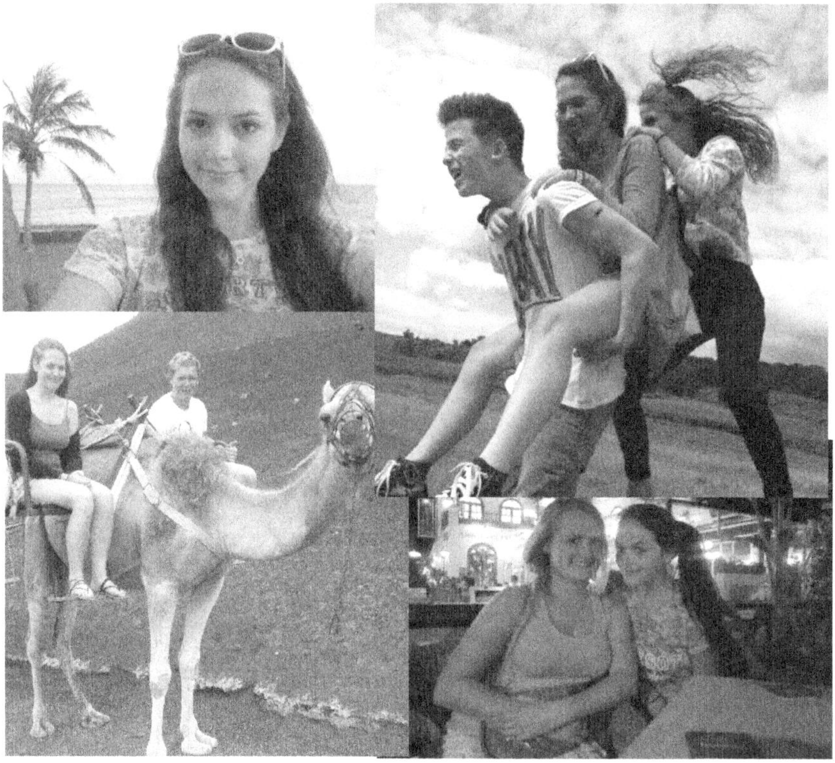

'I know this spark inside will turn into a fire'.
- Cimorelli, worth the fight.

# Chapter Five
## Ana takes the wheel.

As term started, we received our exam results and despite having exercised excessively on study leave where I was exercising to the point my body would just buckle to the floor and I had no fuel to keep my brain going... I managed to pass my GCSE's. Study leave was the first time that I fainted, I felt weak and dizzy and knew a little glass of water would ease it so I went to get one from the kitchen, my ears rang and my body began to sweat and I remember just turning into jelly as I fell to the floor. The glass smashed and my sister shouted from the other room 'what the hell was that', luckily I am **VERY** clumsy and I have always been so I sat on the floor as my sight fizzled back and my body stopped twitching and replied 'just dropped a glass sorry'. I was an addict. An addict to the empty pit, to the sick look, to the fainting and to everything else that came along with it, I was an addict. Anorexia was my heroin.

It is easy to ignore the fact that Eating disorders are addictive, perhaps because they are already so misunderstood by a society that sees them as 'phases' or for 'rich white girls. Eating disorders do not discriminate in any way, they do not care about your race, religion, gender, sex or age. They can occur for many reasons not just trauma and they are not in any way about vanity or an obsession with being like supermodels like many would have you believe.

I named this chapter 'Ana takes the wheel' for two reasons, number one being that I turned my back on my religion, believing that God didn't care about me, hating that he gave me this burden to bare. I resented him and I resented the fact that I was still alive, but did not have the courage to end my life. Yep, that is me the whining, self-pitying fool! Number two being the inevitable car crash caused by the bitch that was Anorexia. After my GCSE's and the summer break I spiralled and began engaging in 'tricks' to manipulate those around me into believing a) that I was ok and b) I was eating. My scale tricks on the other hand, did not work for long and despite the endless quantity of water chugged or the endless amount of heavy things buried in my hair or clothes that number just kept on falling.

I was sent back to Oakham house in the October and to be honest them turning me away beforehand probably damaged me so much more than if they had just treated me for the obvious issue. Upon my return to the Eating Disorder clinic we met my 'therapist' I put that in quotes because her constant focus was on that bloody weight graph or calories consumed only making it worse. I really disagree with how they treated me in terms of the constant focus being on BMI, weight and intake which would only lead me to be competitive with myself. How much could I lose before my next weigh in, if it went up would that make me a failure? would they think I was ok? The focus should not be on the weight but the situation. Slowly but surely, I began to lose friends, bit by bit the letters of encouragement written became letters from old friends that Ana pushed away. There is nothing that can ever prepare you for the pain and loneliness that Anorexia brings you, what is infuriating is that letting her in starts as a friendship but then it quickly sours, you are pulling away from her claws, fighting tooth and nail to break free from this demon consuming you but at the same time, you do not want to leave.

This brings us to early 2014 roughly and I was now the girl in the beanie, Ice cold and manipulating everyone around me, Turner would try and sit with me at lunch but the most I would eat was a celery stick. Wednesday would catch me running between periods (the joys of free periods in college AS levels) as my trainers found a new home in my Art draw, My grades were slipping fast and this only exacerbated my illness because I just felt like such a failure. I was not good at anything, everyone else was doing better than me (of course they were because I was daydreaming about food or adding calories up in the back of my notebooks instead of paying attention or doing the work).

I was going for toilet breaks and doing laps around the school before returning, my cuts were only increasing as my weight decreased and my expectations rose. Eilish ( one of my closest friends back then) was so helpful in history and I really cannot thank her enough for all the times she sat with me explaining what had been done whilst I had been off at therapy or off sick. Unfortunately, this was definitely what ended our friendship, I think she may have just gotten fed up of the illness to be fair and I do not blame her but I wish her all the best she is an amazing girl.

"Come on Chlo, just eat a little" my friend Amy said, Eilish and Chloe watched from across the table. My boyfriend at the time stared at me as I ate one potato ball, my gut churned and I could feel the fat sticking to my digestive system, bubbling under my skin. I waited a few minutes until the attention moved from me and to Sophie and got up to purge the poison, Wednesday ran after me where she heard me vomit and began to shout at me through the toilet door, Abby was in the bathroom at the time and so she was yelling too. I totally zoned her out, as I left the cubicle to the sinks where I pinched my cheeks and washed my hands off, she stared at me in shock.

I never really purged after that and it was only ever chewing gum , I've never binged and I'm not entirely sure as to why as most Anorexic bios I have read describe binging to the point of bursting but I guess people have their own demons and experiences.

Art, the best lesson really because both teachers were amazing, and I was with my closest friends at that point; We stood around the table as Miss C explained what we were doing and then 'crap' I thought and crap being the cause quite literally!! I had begun to abuse laxatives TMI anorexia means pooping is super hard !! anyway I was taking WAY over the recommended dose and I collapsed to the floor clenching my stomach (yet I still thought these were the best things in the world for clearing my system), I didn't want to explode in school, I could think of nothing worse than being in a stall in the school when the consequences of yet another overdose kicked in. It didn't take Wednesday more than two minutes to storm after me as I left the classroom, I was halfway down the stairs when she grabbed my arm 'you're taking laxatives aren't you ?' she was furious but for the first time, at Ana not at me.

She walked me to the medical room where I told Vicky (our school admin at the time and future friend) I was feeling awful and so I went home. We laughed it off as I kept her informed of my uncontrollable pain and discomfort walking home. Have you ever tried walking home whilst sweating and shaking holding in a laxative poop? I do not recommend. Needless to say, that when I got home, I didn't leave the toilet for about an hour maybe more! EMBARASSING.

So... let's get back to the treatment side of my Anorexia, firstly the man who definitely saved my life several times Dr Adcock. I contacted Dr Adcock nearly 8 years ago (or something like that) and Wednesday often rang him when she was concerned. Initially he was not too concerned, but soon things just began to progress and worsen but unlike CAMHS he knew to weigh me in only sun top and leggings which really infuriated Ana. I remember the first time he said 'what are we going to do with you' as he told me my Iron levels were low and I had told him how often I was fainting and my intake. I am so thankful for him seeing as he could have dropped me whenever, but he stayed fighting with me.

CAMHS was terrible where I was, and it was renowned for it. I think CAMHS is pretty much potluck, it depends where you are in the country as a friend of mine had a much better team. I can only hope that they have improved since my treatment. So, the general run down of my appointments was as follows:

1. Get weighed in the stupid tiny room.
2. Blood Pressure.
3. Sit in a room in silence for half of the appointment.
4. Remain silent whilst Mum and K (ugh) talked and told me I was killing myself. I sort of zombified myself or at least let the demon stare into thin air eyes glazed over with disinterest.
5. Watch as the bloody weight graph came out and she showed me where I was on THE LINE (I hated that line).

Now I personally believe the intense focus on weight and food can be more triggering than helpful and for me as I previously said; I saw this chart as a competition with myself, believing that if it went up at all then I had failed, aiming to drop every single week but with that came the guilt of getting worse and seeing my Mum in pain.

So, every visit went the same way and it always ended one of two ways... Mum being angry and screaming at me in the car 'do you want to die Chloe? Do you?' and so on or... me holding a grudge and refusing to speak. I was a shadow of the girl I once was, I was so weak and under my beanie my hair was falling out, I was the media image now and people knew by looking at me that I was sick and in a disturbed way ... I liked it. It meant I was thin.

Dr Adcock saw me regularly and, in all fairness, even though the answer was always 'it's malnourishment' or 'because you aren't eating Chloe' he was so reassuring. I was the emaciated girl Ana wanted me to be, but it was not enough, I was desperate to lose more and addicted to watching the numbers fall. I was still not thin enough (looking back at photos it frustrates me that I was always striving to be thinner, even when there was not much left. My once flowing thick hair was now brittle, falling out and breaking off making it shorter and shorter, it was entirely lifeless just like the head it sat upon.

I couldn't comfort Mum as I did as a child, my caring personality was gone, Ana was in control, she had possessed my body to the point that I was numb to my crying Mum, a scene that makes me feel like such a heartless bitch to this day. Letting Ana in had turned me into a shell, I shut the door to everyone who loved and cared about me. My emotions were gone, I was numb and isolated from the world, I was merely surviving in a world that was always turning and no matter how hard I tried I just couldn't let go, the way hunger made me feel was just too comforting, my favourite being the high, floating above the world but then there's the dreaded pain inside , guilt and utter disgust when you eat that extra hundred calories in hopes the dizziness will subside.

Every time I ate, I felt like I could feel the food sticking to me, bubbling into fat under my skin, it was so distressing. I had an appointment in July that sticks with me. This was the appointment in which I was told I couldn't go on holiday, because I 'wouldn't get back alive' I was gutted because I was so desperate to go to France and so we went home and I gained a little weight. We went on holiday, but alas when we returned home my already rigid diet went back to restriction. I had an amazing holiday though, we laughed and me and Dean made a tarte Tatin together, picking our own apples from the grounds of our chateau apartment. Danielle and I rekindled our relationship and were talking into all hours of the night, I felt like me! I ate a macaron or two (my favourite) and I even had some meals out and about but that soon all ended.

October 2014 and I remember staring out of the window, the sun on my face as I blocked out my Mother's pleas. I have always loved doing this, looking at that burning ball of yellow that makes everyone so happy. I prayed for an escape as I zone back in like a scene from Harry Potter as they zap in from the portkey. 'Do you want to die Chlo?' what a strange thing to ask, why would my Mum ask me that? Why would I want to lose all those I love? Why would I want to hurt them? 'No Mummy, I don't want to die, I just can't stop. Mummy I can't stop' I wailed back at her, we screech up at Brocks Hill park, a park near whereas a little girl I tapped my little feet away at dance class in the building next door.

'Get out' mum said, I honestly thought she was kicking me out, but she too slammed the door behind her. We walk towards the hill, my legs shaking 'come on then mum ushered' I got teary-eyed as I remembered the curly haired happy little girl who would run up this hill to the park on Dance breaks. There Mum told me how she felt, and it shocked me, she said things that to this day will haunt me, but we agreed to leave that conversation at the bench and never discuss it again.

We had left perhaps the worst appointment we had ever had. My weight had plummeted so much that week and K told me they were going to admit me ! she also felt the need to tell my Mum to get used to having one daughter and that the NHS wasn't going to 'waste money on a corpse', I know right ... supportive ! She had the audacity to say to Mum 'now's the time where it'd be good for you to get on board'! Oh, my goodness I have never seen Mum speechless, but she had been asking for months 'what can I do?' and they had said nothing. We left embarking on the 'Maudsley Method' which is 'Family based treatment' where Mum would be in control and 'participate' 'positively' in my recovery. Mum had saved me from admission again, not to mention that the closest bed was **SHEFFIELD!** Of which was over an hour away.

Mum was now my inpatient unit; I was on bed rest and CAMHS had told us I could only go out if I was in a wheelchair as I could not exercise. I was infuriated by the idea because at this point, I was convinced I still was not sick enough. I did not care that those once sparkling eyes were now hollow, all I could see was that I needed to lose more weight.

## A mother's point of view:
CAMHS, how I hated that place! All I can say is thank god for smart phones because Candy crush gave me what little distraction I could get whilst Chloe was in for her therapy. I was hoping and praying she had not lost again, my phone gave me some distraction from feeling that people were staring at me, feeling sorry for me... something I have always despised. Immediate bed rest was the result of this appointment, I had refused to admit her knowing that she would not survive away from us. Her weight was dangerously low, and they told me she would not make it to the end of the year.

Bed rest it was, I would take her food up all day and every day and she sleeps, people visit and chat with her whilst I am at work. My birthday came around and we had a day off, I let her come into town with us to shop and had lunch before heading home for a party. What a great day it was, free, easy and relaxing, it felt normal but then CAMHS rolled around and she had lost weight again. They told me she was doing too much and 1800 was not enough to sustain her even at bare minimal 'why didn't they tell me this' I thought, I was furious. I always felt like I had to do my own research and at this point I was scouring everywhere for more information.

## A best friend's point of view:
There was a shift in Chloe at this point, she became fully engulfed in her disorder and as much as I hated her for it, I could not leave, she needed me, and I loved her too much. I ended up running from college to her house to pick her up off the floor after she had worked out too much, collapsed and was too weak to stand back up without fainting again.

Me and Chlo have this special bond after all of our trials and tribulations, in the face of Ana I could have run or stuck by my best friend and I can't imagine not being there for her. The amount of times I picked up the phone to ring Dr Adcock when I knew she wouldn't, or hiding all her coke zero to get her to eat (this did not work at all ). I will never laugh as much as I did when she was texting me on her walk home having taking those laxatives, we found humour in the pain because without it, life would have been constantly dark and so whilst many don't understand our humour (initially Josh didn't when they first got together) we know in a way it saved our friendship. It stopped Ana taking our friendship, it allowed me to laugh it off and in times when my own mental health could not handle it I would distance myself, but not for long because she needed me by her side to fight. It broke my heart watching my best friend disappear from her bubbly curly haired self to a hollow shell.

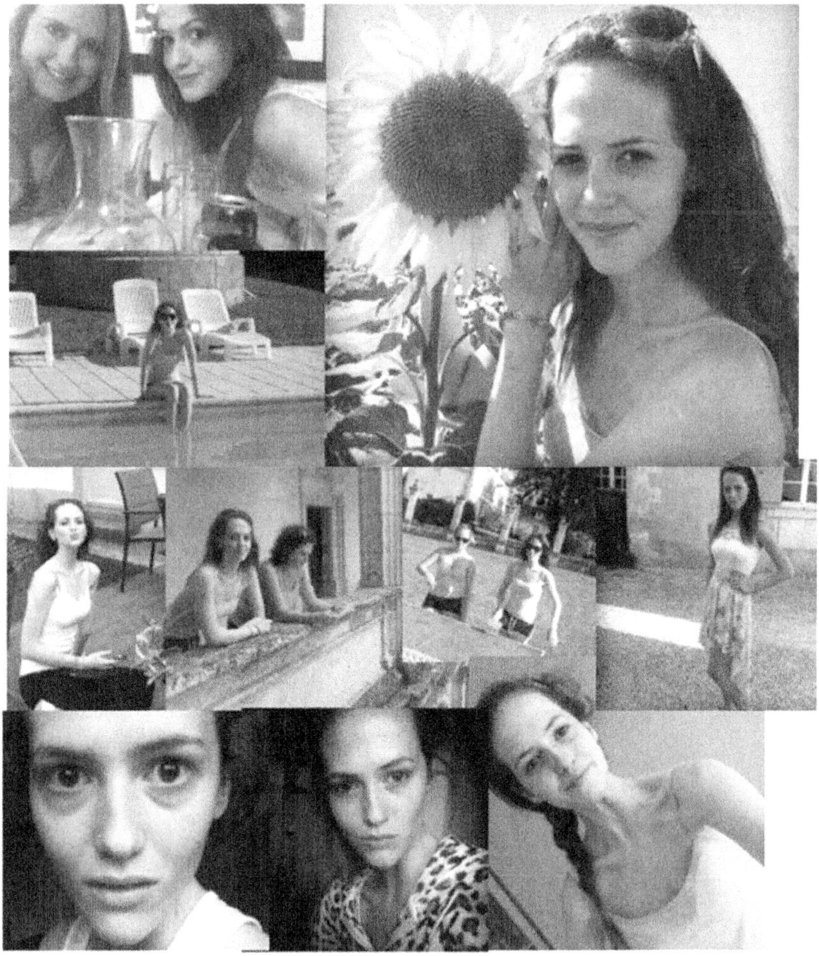

'Your body is the house you grew up in, how dare you try to burn it to the ground'.
- Unknown.

# Chapter Six
## The battle begins.

1,800 perhaps was not enough. However, it would soon come out that whilst I was on bed rest I was in fact hiding the food under my bed, chewing and spitting it into bags or just hiding it in bags (gross I know). I needed to be watched 24/7 because this illness is so manipulative. I digress, I agreed to change, and I start bed rest 24/7. I felt so guilty and fat laying there all day and I felt more alone than ever as I listened to my family downstairs but that was exactly how Ana wanted me to feel, she was my only friend or so I thought.

I remember clearly when Wednesday came around after college to visit, she came with my 'boyfriend' at the time and Amy and I sat drinking my 'fortisip' with them, their faces were a picture of pride and relief and it killed me. Now, I feel terrible about this but I would sneak down to the garage and empty my fortisip's out replacing them with water ( FYI Vanilla and Apricot are the best flavours, Mocha, coffee and banana made me feel sick!) and sealing them back up again. SO MANIPULATIVE but also in my defence kinda clever? I was so proud of myself for fooling everyone, but it was myself I was fooling, thinking I would be ok to carry on the way I was. They were so proud of me but all I could think about was this game of numbers, this project I had embarked on this game of lies and manipulation as I edged towards what Ana wanted me to be but the truth was she wanted me dead all along, if only I could've seen it.

'It won't happen to me', 'just a little more', the phrases I so strongly believed but now it was happening to me. Agreeing to change was the hardest decision I ever made but as my hero says, 'recovery doesn't get a day off' (Demi obviously). I had in the past embarked on what I call 'recovery-maybe-ish-nah-I'll stop here's' there had been some really dark moments leading up to this, one being carving 'FAT' into my wrist another taking an overdose that Sophie luckily interrupted midway with a phone call (Thankyou Sophie) but this, this was without a doubt my darkest. I had pushed so many people away, my baby cousin who was and still is such a light in my life eventually got pushed out too, she was 5. I could not play with her I was just too tired; I could not lift her because my arms were just too frail, and I can never forgive myself for that.

Maudsley was so difficult and one of the reasons is that Anorexia is **VERY** possessive so you can imagine she was not thrilled when someone else took the reins. The following appointment I had lost weight (as previously mentioned) and Mum pleaded with me telling me she would do anything, yes bribery. An incentive and what was that incentive? A kitten, we told Dr Coffey (my psych at Oakham who was so lovely) and she was so optimistic and supportive and then we told K... well we left **CAMHS** laughing for once, it felt like we had given her therapy this time, she shut the idea down telling Mum I'd just relapse again, she almost thrived off of me being sick and the idea of me getting better seemed to anger her. Mum told K that she would simply rehome the kitten (if my Mum says she will do something, she will) if I relapsed. I think one of my biggest incentives to get better was to rekindle my relationship with my sister again, she had caught me exercising on bed rest before this appointment and lost it. I feel terrible for putting her through it all, she was at uni at the time, so it really must have taken a toll (Sorry D, I am so, so sorry).

Once we got home I started my 'Pixie Dust challenge', my obsession with Peter Pan growing up led us to use 'Faith, Trust and Pixie Dust' as our new motto and we did fear food challenges named 'pixie dust challenge', the theme being because I had chosen to call my future kitten Pixie. Mum and I came to the agreement that it would be best for me to be watched whilst eating, I did this after one night in particular, my family have always said that those we love that we lose become stars in the sky, so I lay in bed with the curtains ajar staring at the stars. I found Nanny and Auntie Rachel and felt such guilt, I thought to myself that Auntie Rachel would be furious as she could not fix her heart, but I could fix mine. I looked at the baby monitor which would tell my parents if I exercised and thought 'who am I?' this was not me; I wasn't a liar or a manipulator, I wasn't Chloe anymore. I finally noted their pain, their pleads, I stared at the stars and whispered 'enough' to myself and that marked my journey to recovery.

Instagram, I don't know how it is now but when I was recovering, I had an amazing group of friends who were also going through recovery and there was no competition between us only motivation. I made friends with a girl named Emily and she honestly was one of my closest confidants, I remember when we first met after I was allowed to walk again, and it was amazing! We had Starbucks and shopped and even had some Froyo which I cannot get around here, so Cambridge was the best meeting spot for that.

I became stronger and despite being unable to do my A levels (I passed AS, and I am not sure how!) I was getting there, Mrs S was amazing and arranged for me to complete my art A level from home and I passed, I am so proud of myself for that. Things were gradually improving but then Mum went on a residential trip with the school in September and things went well to an extent. However, my Anorexic behaviours kicked in a bit more and the little control I had went away as I began to cut out foods. Luckily, mum had written me a note for every day and that kept me going. My Dad was amazing with it all after he had lost it all those months ago and could not understand why he couldn't just force feed me. Now he would cradle me and hug me as I cried with anxiety and my panic attacks increased. I remember spilling out that I knew why people killed themselves and this terrified my parents it is also when my suicidal tendencies and thoughts began.

Mum returned and knew I needed help so CAMHS put us in touch with the Crisis team. This time felt like the scariest and darkest time of my life, looking back I think this is when my other mental illness began to show itself. I could not function, the thoughts just occupied and pulled me into my first major depression. I was utterly numb, it felt as though the real Chloe was chained in a cage at the back of my brain in the dark, cold and scared. At this point I think it was the very first time I wished I was admitted because I didn't want to keep hurting people, either that or I wanted to die.

Off we went to CAMHS YET again , it was the biggest chore in my life at this point and I can actually remember this meeting which proves how pivotal it was seeing as I couldn't tell my left from rights , ups from downs at this point. I saw my Mum broken, for the first time. I think I had just enough in me to help me see that it was not just me lifeless and hurt anymore, it was her too... game on Ana, no one hurt my Mummy. At that meeting I honestly thought Mum was going to let them take me at this point, I thought at this point looking at her drained face that she was done but she was not. She later revealed that she came the closet she had ever been to actually giving up in believing in me and I hate that she got to that point.

The red book... ah yes, the book of torment, the book that recorded every sin, every violation to my body, what did it record? **CALORIES.** I was now being watched 24/7, my big sister Danielle, Grandma, Grace, Auntie Anita, everyone would come when they could whilst mum was at work, it is like we all united against this demon. I do remember seeing my Grandmas face sink as I declined her egg and cress sandwiches, a childhood favourite. Wednesday ended up having to babysit me! How embarrassing, being 17 and being babysat by your best friend. I remember thinking, we should be out at parties, eating out and making memories yet there she sat watching me fight with each bite to come back from rock bottom.

Whilst Mum was working, she would ring me 3-5 times just to check in and make sure I was still alive, I guess. I was so exhausted all I remember is the tears and the pleas from family members and friends. I was missing Brownies ( I'm a Girlguiding leader) and so when Auntie Anita came by to pick up Mum she made absolute sure that I was looking at her when she said ' don't you dare do this to your mum', now Auntie Anita isn't exactly subtle and by God can she scare you when she snaps and although she didn't really get it , she got through to Chloe.

## A mother's point of view:

Dr. Adcock, what an amazing man, Chloe trusted and still trusts him entirely, he is blunt but in a good way. He was checking her heart and warning us of it slowing so with another book I began to log her BP, if it fell, we had to go to the hospital. Once we did have to and when we came out with the 'all clear' Chloe had just shrugged it off, how can she have been so calm? I think her attitude remained 'it won't happen to me', what else would it take to show her she was dying? She was killing herself and we couldn't fight this for her. My baby girl, with the curly blonde hair, always smiling and laughing. In love with all things yellow, my little girl who makes the whole room smile and laugh when she walks in. Where is she? My baby girl who was once so in love with life, enthusiastic about everything she does, gets up when she falls, gives everything her all and isn't happy until she succeeds, my stubborn little madam. Lost. These qualities that should be good helped my baby girl succeed at the deadliest game she could play... Anorexia.

Family life was hell, Phil and Danielle could feel the tension, Anorexia encompassed us both. My Mum worried tremendously for me, but I had no time to rest, my little girl was dying in front of me, she needed back up. Since CAMHS had proved useless to us, I took it upon myself to read about this disease to have at least some ammunition in this battle. When we did go to CAMHS after my residential trip I found myself looking down at myself I was scared and for a brief moment I thought 'let them take her, you need to rest'... I felt an overwhelming relief and then snap! Back to reality, this was my battle too, we became one.

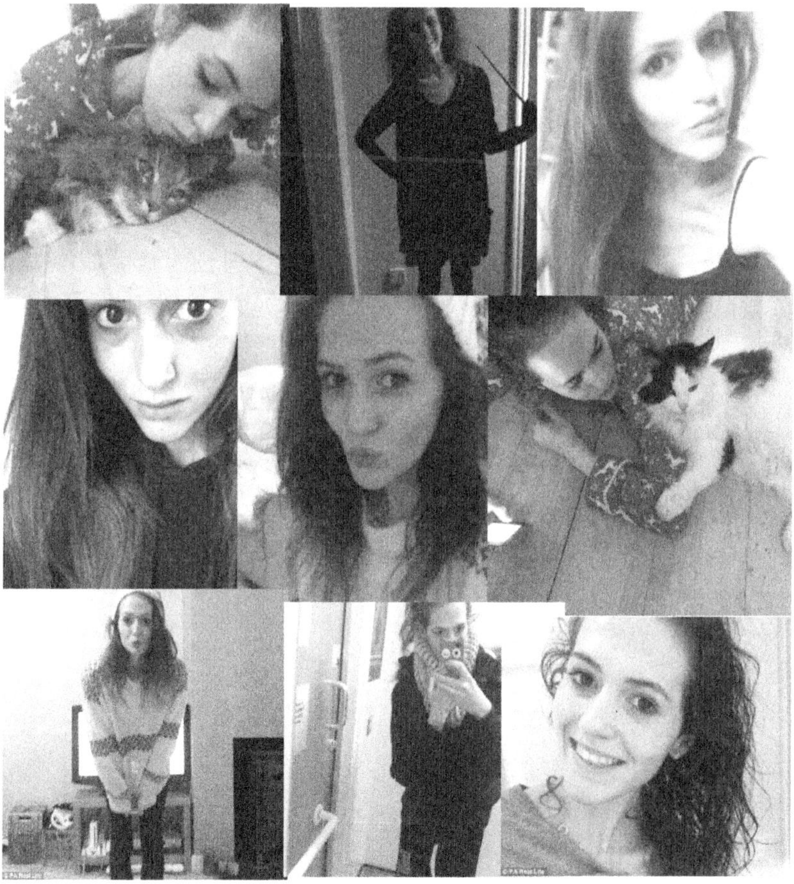

'Knowing is better than wondering, waking is better than sleeping, and even the biggest failure, even the worst, beats the hell out of never trying.'
-Izzie Stevens, Grey's Anatomy

# Chapter Seven
## We are one.

So, Mum got time off work and that seemed to work, we ate together which limited the number of tricks Anorexia could pull and she NEVER left me alone. Looking back it was for the best and allowed her to gain full control which was such a relief, but I do not think I have ever hated my Mum except for then, however the burning hatred was purely Ana. I could feel the food sticking to my organs, bubbling under my skin turning to fat but there was no escape, Mum was too knowledgeable now. Anorexia could not get in, she was locked out, it was just me and Mum. We watched TV and films all the things that pamper you and make you feel better, Mum would tickle my back for me (although she said it made her cringe because of my skeletal frame but I was often very distant and just slept.

I felt like I was missing out on so much, especially in August, we went to Dads kit car end of season camp and I only stayed for the day because I was just too sick to stay overnight and Auntie Emma (not technically my auntie) and Nick were amazing with me. Nick sat me down in his caravan and let me just rant before giving it to me straight the damage he could see and then a pep talk.

Auntie Emma just made me laugh and showered me with love and support (she always has). I was gutted when I had to leave, I was missing out on spending time with those I did not see very often, yet another restriction as a result of Anorexia. Yet I knew I was not me anymore because all of the foods available that I would years ago have tried to brave (hog roast) I could not even consider, I couldn't consider anything but a salad or soup (I was very rigid in recovery and my diet was pretty much one thing or another per meal, I was not adventurous). My prison was that was once inside my body was now outside as well, I was side-lined from life (I used a sports reference there which I am quite proud of!).

FOMO had nothing on what I was feeling but in October 2014 it was time for Mum to go back to work, but her boss, who is absolutely amazing bless him, agreed for me to go in with Mum as I was often in for helping out anyway. It was hard at first especially letting go of a project I had worked so hard on and I resented Mum so much but also sitting in a staff room whilst other people ate things I could only dream of as I dug into my special K PLAIN porridge was torture, I did not and still do not understand how people can eat so carefreely. The diet talk was the worst but the staff (who are like my own second family) adapted and began talking about other things, to an extent I think it was good for them to step away from the diet culture too. I was so exhausted of this constant battle of wills, trying to please Mum, but also trying to not let go completely of Ana that I mainly just sat in silence at Kirsty's desk, attached to the heater, cocooned in my endless layers. This was a tell as to how much Ana had taken as I love children, I love teaching and working with them, but I was just a shell. Children are amazing therapy, they do not see anything other than you, they accept so easily and soon I began to realise I was not alone anymore, every day I did not just have my family on my side I now had Kirsty, Nicole, Angie, Debbie and so many more in my corner too.

Treat Thursday, something that Mums work has done for years. It was terrifying and as much as I wanted to be brave I just couldn't, Nicole , Kirsty and Angie would often joke about having more because it was just one day as a way of telling me it was ok to eat these treats. However, to me it was a table of inevitable torture and then , just like that I leant forward and took a cookie that Kirsty had bought in for her turn, I still remember the staff room getting quieter and then the staff cheering me on, they were like my own little army. I then proceeded to have a panic attack which poor Kirsty walked in on and was not sure how to handle it, but she did an amazing job and then sent for mum. At this point I had stopped filling my fortisip's with water, partly because I had no chance to and I was nearly caught far too often by staff coming into the kitchen.

Fear food Fridays, this started on Instagram and mums work took it upon themselves to make it a treat day in which we would all go into Blaby (the little village) and get lunch. This is when I was still restricting so my idea of a treat was often apple crisps and sushi... yeah... Ok Chlo. Kirsty, Angie and Nicole would set me challenges and I would send them videos or photos of me completing them. Slowly, bit by bit Chloe was returning. There was a little girl in year 1 who I ended up bonding with pretty fast, it was the first time I was allowed out of Mums class into another and she just attached herself to me, she was always smiling, cheeky and had curly blonde hair, in a way it was like looking at a little me and I found myself cheering up and engaging, I even ate a banana, she brought me, (A HUGE FEAR) from the snack tray at break. My trance was breaking and the girl who would be too sick to walk about and then snap into an exercise frenzy suddenly disappeared and weirdly I was feeling weaker.

If I could tell someone recovering anything it would be that things definitely get worse before they get better physically but that does not mean it is not worth it and I'll get to that a bit later. Mums longest work friend Angie eventually got comfortable enough to take me out just us two to walk the dogs, some animal therapy in her time off. The thing is that mums' friends will still make time for me today which is something I will always be thankful for. We chatted about pointless stuff and laughed at the dog as she trotted through the mud, this was perhaps the longest walk I had done in so long and despite how bloody cold it was the cold air hitting my face was a memory that will stay with me as the time I started to feel a bit more like Chloe again.

By the evenings the day would catch up with me, I'd often end up huddled in my corner in the kitchen shaking like a cornered animal, Dad holding me tight until my panic attacks eased and arms bleeding from scratching at them. I felt dreadful, I felt like I was lost and trapped.

Pixie. I started to use Kirsty's laptop to browse sites looking for my kitten as the weight started to go on, I was determined she would be white with blue eyes, I don't know how many cats I shoved in Mum and Kirsty's faces, but the search began (it would go on for some time). My temper however had turned, I would snap and when I did I was a real bitch, I was nasty and I wish I could take back what I once said, but people just ignored it knowing it was Ana. Danielle treated me to getting my nails done when I was getting better because I think our relationship was finally starting to mend, we would now go to the cinema together or just chat and it was like things had gone back to how things once were.

Little did we know this temper was an insight into what was coming mental health wise. I was starting to thrive again, and I actually started to want to fight and then it happened one of the most horrible things I had to miss out on ... New York City. My dream, New York City embedded itself into my heart at just five-years-old, I could have been booking my place on this flight with her: she had told me she wanted to take me, but I was just too sick. Danielle was pretty much done with her degree and she had a trip to NYC of which I was missing out on, the best girl's trip there could have been, a chance to bond again. I looked down towards the doors and two girls from my school were booking a holiday and all I could think was that I wasn't allowed anywhere alone; I had no job to even fund a trip, I was frozen in time as the world kept spinning.

Kirsty began to give me more jobs and responsibilities around the classroom and lets face it, we all need that one blunt friend to set us straight and that was Kirsty, she knew it was hard and she didn't fully understand but she made time to, she also made time to show me how stupid diets are. Nicole would lend an ear whenever I needed it, I would sit and talk to her whilst sketching the school play set for Lisa, she was very good at understanding my anxiety and both of them would calm me at lunch and break. Angie has known me since I was tiny, and she often shared her new recipes with me and talk me through her AMAZING lunches so that one day if I was brave enough, I would eat them. I think one of the main things I am grateful for is that they were not just there for me, they were there for Mum 24/7 and they still are.

Gradually I started to feel better physically but I just could not get on board mentally and the little tricks were still present. I was still cutting corners and manipulating the process where I could. I could not bring myself to let go, I could not let go of the years of work, pain and tears. I did know one thing and it was that I missed me, I missed smiling, I missed laughing, I missed my families smiles and I missed being the silly life of the party making everyone laugh. I wished that I could recover but stay bones, I wish I could eat but, it just wasn't that easy, I couldn't bring myself to put each bite in and the chewing just prolonged the pain. I think that is why I preferred small and soft food instead of anything too chewy. I do remember clearly the first dinner I all but finished, I remember the look on my Mum and Dads faces as I got up sheepishly. Fish pie. Mums homemade fish pie , it was the first thing I could taste , the first thing my body really let in and I didn't feel like it was rejecting it, my body felt warm, homely and at peace with the process.

**A mother's point of view:**

Maudsley method was working and at last I felt a little in control it was basically inpatient treatment at home, she would eat what was given to her which had been portioned and calorie counted then she would be watched 24/7 the only difference was she got a say in what food she would eat. Some days Chlo would smile and it would be her, her eyes would light up. It would bring tears to my eyes and other days she would be a real Bitch, nasty with a short temper and she truly was awful. I am a red head and Chloe has my fiery temper too but the things she would say would leave me stunned. When did my little girl turn into this nasty demon? Her weight was still critical, but she had accepted that I wasn't going to stand by and watch her die but I couldn't help her when the pain of recovery hit in, not the physical but the mental. She was utterly disgusted in herself and now it was me V Ana with poor Chloe stuck between a rock and a hard place.

My work colleagues were mini councillors to her, telling her some home truths and helping her brave certain foods. I was finally able to do my job again with ease, knowing I could see her and watch for Ana's claws, I could protect her. It's awful when you can't trust your own child but over time our routine was perfected but she still didn't want to get better, I wanted to climb inside her brain and beat the crap out of the nasty bitch making my daughter feel 'unworthy of life'.

'Christmas is most truly Christmas when we celebrate it by giving the light of love to those who need it most'.
-Ruth Carter Stapleton

# Chapter Eight
## Elfing about.

Christmas is and always has been my favourite time of year, from baking cookies with my Dad (his speciality) to the warm DVD days in front of our log fire, putting the decorations up to music and the general magic surrounding it.

It was November (2014) before we knew it and the Maudsley Method was starting to work, the weight was going on and my heart was improving, my periods would come back really early with a still very low BMI (I'm very grateful that my body trusted me and let them come back so early) and I was starting to heal. In the past, I had worked seasonally as a Christmas elf (since I was 14) and I was desperate for some independence again, desperate to be at work and watch as the kids met Santa, opened their gifts and saw the reindeers. My response to questions were always quick so the kids got to have full discussions with me about Santa's life and our lives as elves! I loved the atmosphere I loved listening to the kids Christmas lists and picking the best toy for them.

However CAMHS (you guessed it), weren't so keen, but yet as expected, they put all the pressure on Mum, 'it's up to you Mrs Shelton', in other words 'if she gets worse it's your fault' . To my utter amazement, Mum agreed to let me work so long as I was at a steady (NUMBER ALERT) seven stone. Daddy also played a huge part in this decision telling me and Mum that there was no point fighting if I felt like there was nothing to live for and work would provide a purpose for me, something I loved doing and most importantly a purpose and a distraction.

The thought itself of being Seven stone terrified me, and I so wanted to be busy (to lose weight) and earn some money. Mum was one step ahead of Anorexia, as she always was at this point and told me that if I was going to do this, I had to come outside and meet either her or Dad in the car and eat my lunch supervised. Anorexia was less than impressed about losing this prime opportunity, but I agreed and, in a way, felt a sense of relief that she had been a step ahead of Ana.

Sidenote, relinquishing control to Mum was the hardest thing I had to do but in a way, I felt an overwhelming sense of relief, I felt like someone could be responsible for my decisions now and the control or lack thereof that I had would now no longer exist. Ultimately it was me being freed from Ana, cutting the cord so to speak.

The thing was, we had so many other factors to contend with as I began work, the drop in weather meant my body was trying harder to keep warm and so I had to eat more (this did NOT go well) and all the once joyful memories of Christmas became terrors. How could I survive surrounded by all these people pushing fatty foods on me? Why couldn't they stop now? I was not as thin or as sick so why can't I just stay the same?!

I worked mostly all of my shifts but had to admit defeat a few times when it was too much, too cold or I was too weak and so I would have to miss the shift but I was doing it . Yes, I lost a little weight but as the Christmas period came in, I was able to sleep more as school finished and boy did, I sleep! I was so cold it was really the only time I could be warm! That is one thing I think needs to be addressed, yes, a lot of Anorexics wear baggy clothes to hide but also because it is BLOODY COLD.

November was our starting month and our timetables came through, 'great' I thought as I glanced down at my sheet which stated 'training' above a teenage boys name who probably 'doesn't even care about the kids' and will probably 'be a pain in my ass'. Oh, how wrong I was! Granted he was hard work to train up, but he was not a teenage spotty annoying boy, he was 17 the same as me and I remember his shy smile as he met me. As a little girl as I previously mentioned, I loved the film 'practical magic' and as I mentioned I 'cast a spell' just like Sally Owens (Sandra Bullock) that I would only fall in love with someone who had 'bluey green eyes'. Extremely specific I know! Then there it was, eye contact and low and behold BLUEY GREEN EYES!! I think my parents knew I was falling way before I did and I remember Danielle saying, 'you talk a lot about Josh, he makes you happy'.

Josh was shy at first and his brown curls flopped about his forehead as he rushed from one side of the workshop to the other, but he was so kind. He saw me as a person, he knew I was Anorexic, but he still offered me chocolate or a cookie, he'd offer me a cup of tea and when he realised I wouldn't have any of it, he used to come back with his tea and a mug of boiling water 'just have this, it'll keep you warm'. I remember his horror when he dropped the present down Santa's chimney too early! He looked at me with these 'shit please help' eyes and luckily, I was able to fix it before anyone noticed (you owe me!).

Suddenly, I didn't want to look sick anymore (that's what is so disturbing about this illness, you don't care that you look sick it acts as a certification that you're a 'good' anorexic). Josh and I would mess about with all the kid toys having a real laugh, that belly laugh that you get where you laugh so much your tummy cramps. Josh added me on Facebook that New year and before I knew it, he had invited me out ... TO NANDOS!

So, NYE 2014 was when I self-harmed for the first time in months and it ... was... bad. I was terrified to tell Mum, but she reacted so calmly, she was mad, but you could tell it was to Ana and not to me, I went to the Drs for steristrips and a proper check over the next day and in early January Danielle left for NYC. I text Josh the whole time to and from dropping her at the airport and he was so calming about it all, I think that is when I thought that this guy was not just pittying me. Danielle kept me updated throughout the whole trip, I think she wished I could have gone too but alas, we would get our chance and the wait would be so worth it.

January 24th, 2015 came around and it was time, I was so nervous, and I was not entirely sure whether this was a date or not. Nando's, I thought 'how the hell am I going to do this? I can't do this; I should just cancel' but Wednesday was in my corner yet again. She pushed me out of my little nest of safety and trusted I would fly, and I did!! I ATE MY WHOLE MEAL, my stomach felt like it was about to rupture and albeit I did not have a huge meal, but it was a massive achievement. I even let Josh fill my drink up for me (sore subject) and he made me laugh as he promptly drank his drink and mine because he had ordered 'extra hot'. He held my hand before food came and straight up just cleared things up... he said he wanted me to be his girlfriend and I was head over heels!! What's more, we went to the cinema afterwards to watch 'The Theory of Everything' and I ATE SWEETS as well as my Nando's, when I came home I remember grinning ear to ear as I said to mum 'he's my boyfriend'.

Josh would be so supportive with my Anorexia, encouraging me to eat fear foods and eating them with me so it felt normal. I was so nervous about meeting his parents (Peta and Jon), I wondered if they would hate that he was dating someone with so many issues, but they accepted me into their family straight away, Gloria (Josh's Nan) also accepted me and was always making me feel comfortable around food. Pretty soon, our families became each other's, and our relationship continued to blossom.

Peta did us a chocolate fondue once and I remember I was so terrified, but we sat on the floor in Josh's room and I felt like such a rebel! He was making me brave. We watched NCIS and eventually he got me into Star Trek, we would see each other every Wednesday, Friday, Saturday and Sunday sleeping over Fridays and Saturdays alternately and things just felt normal. I felt like a normal young adult in a normal relationship. Albeit I gave him plenty of outs and pushed him out a lot, but he always found a way back in and Ana HATED that.

## A mother's point of view:

Before I knew it, November was here. Oh, my goodness, Christmas would be upon us before we knew it. Now we had added issues such as extra food to keep her warm but also the adverts about indulgence and diets were beginning to kick in and I could see what a negative impact this was having on Chloe. She has often spoken to me since about how that time of year is the worst in terms of triggering TV shows 'diet' this and 'bad foods' that. Me and Phil would ensure we got her attention away from the TV should any of those adverts come on and in terms of the car... we always have the Christmas CD in as soon as the celebrations start so the radio wasn't a problem.

Christmas would bring major challenges for Chloe. Deep breath I thought to myself, off we go. The most important hurdle and battle I had that month was at CAMHS (again!) about Chloe's Elf job, 'she absolutely loves it' I told them 'it gives her a real buzz'. CAMHS told us she should not work, she would lose weight, her body was not ready, and it was too cold etc, etc... Then the famous line that this woman would constantly throw 'well, Mrs Shelton, the final decision is yours' in other words... if she dies, we warned you, yeah thanks.

Chloe, Phil and I had long chats, she was desperate to work and so we agreed, it was something to work for and a goal. So, the deal was drawn up! Chloe had to gain consecutively over two weeks and I had the power at any point to say 'no' if I thought she was not coping and the final stipulation, she would meet me or Phil for lunch. Both Phil and I believe we made the right decision even though we were seen as irresponsible but through work was her first major breakthrough, she got friendly with a fellow elf Josh. She has been with him ever since, little did I know how good 2015 was going to be, she lived past Christmas and New Year despite what CAMHS had told us (they were just full of positivity...) and this year was 'our year'. Chlo would be 18, Danielle 21and graduating and me and Phil would have our $25^{th}$ wedding anniversary.

Christmas however was extremely difficult, she lost weight again and admission was looming over us like a thunder cloud, but we were all trying to be normal or as normal as we could be. Christmas at our house isn't much different to others and tradition is crucial, but even the simplest traditions would send her into a panic attack and Christmas morning was no different, stockings were opened and dinner was cooking, we only had Mum over that year as I didn't want too many eyes on Chlo. I found her on the kitchen floor huddled in a ball in her corner, gasping for air and crying silently so as 'not to ruin Christmas'. Chloe has always loved Christmas and suddenly it was torture for her, she used so much energy that day trying to keep positive, smiling and eating. I tried so hard to get her to eat her favourites, but she would always opt for those bloody 29 cal rice cakes! Or cardboard as I call them. I forgot that snippet of information! I had a red book that EVERY calorie had to be logged in, there is not much I don't know anymore.

Boxing day she broke down in tears and told me she could not do it and her intake that day was so low, but we couldn't get her to break, she was in her words 'too fat'. New Year's came around and many family members did and still do crititise me for letting her drink, she got drunk fast with nothing to soak the alcohol up, but we were letting her be NORMAL. Do you know how much I dreamed of that NORMAL phone call from her 'Mum can you pick me up from town? I drank too much, and I forgot my taxi money?' instead of 'Mummy I cannot eat this', 'I want to die' or 'I can't do this'. Which phone call would you prefer? People in white house's etc...

No one, has any idea how awful it is to hear your daughter (or son) , whom you love more than the world itself tell you they want to end it all, they can't cope and Chloe was hating the upset she was causing. As I understand it, guilt also plays a massive part. Behind the image of a coping family was a family screaming and praying for CAMHS's so called 'magic bullet' to hit. We were desperate.

### A boyfriend's point of view:

November was the start of a new job I had worked on a paper round previously and was looking for a way to earn a little bit of money. Our rotas came through and on my first shift I met Chloe, she was going to be the one to show me what to do. In all honesty when I met her, she looked extremely sick and I was told she had an eating disorder, I had never met anyone with Anorexia before and it shocked me.

I treated her like anyone else because she seemed like a lovely person and was helping me at work, to be honest because of her Anorexia she wasn't really that attractive but as I got to know her she shone through, I remember towards the end of work she stopped being able to work.

On New Year's Eve, she sent me a snapchat and we got to talking. We had the same driving instructor and I offered to give her my theory book to study as her sisters was out of date. I had started to take interest in her and I decided to invite her out to lunch at Nando's and a film. Whilst at Nando's I asked her to be my girlfriend and the rest is history.

'We are left with a choice. Either let the guilt throw you back into the behaviour that got you into trouble in the first place or learn from the guilt and do your best to move on.'
- Grey's Anatomy.

# Chapter Nine
# PixieBelle and a Birthday to remember.

At this my recovery was going well and I was still at work with Mum. 'FOUND HER' I loudly whispered to Kirsty in the classroom, to be fair Kirsty had seen so many cats at this point she was probably ready to pull her hair out but she too, approved and seeing as she was not really a cat person that was a blessing ! There had been many potential Pixie's, but she surprised me, and I think that confirmed she was mine; she was not white with blue eyes at all. She was black with orange flecks (little did I know she was a tortie and I would deal with tortitude for years to come!). There had been many possible Pixie's, but fate meant that they all fell through, this Pixie was my baby.

I was not quite at my Pixie weight and I was so furious with myself as I knew she was the one. Yet to my surprise Mum said I could get her if I at least maintained for the next two weeks (I think she saw how hard I had been trying and how dedicated I had become to my recovery). I did gain weight, in fact, I did one better and I GAINED 2.5lbs! CAMHS were shocked that I had actually improved with this 'bribe', it wasn't a bribe though, it was a purpose and so many people on Instagram had been through the same process as animals can really change your life. She would give me a purpose; I could be a cat-mummy and that was such an important responsibility. We already had two, but they were our family cats and were fully independent.

The day we collected her we made a day of it as she was near Hampton Hall which is not exactly a short car trip from Leicester. Although, my parents did end up wanting to pull their hair out the whole way round 'are we nearly done?', 'can we go ?' none of which is like me at all but my little fluff was waiting for her Mummy. I text Josh all day but don't get me wrong I really enjoyed the trip and despite the usual stares and whispers I felt normal even when the woman in the toilets threw me off with her 'are you anorexic?' comment. How dare she? I thought but in a sick way it also reassured me I was not too big yet. I even ate a sandwich! That was a huge deal for me as bread and butter was a massive fear. We took so many photos and had a laugh, me and Daddy were back to our normal selves and we just felt normal.

Overall, it was a lovely day out and we picked my baby girl up on the way home. I was torn between PixieBelle or PixieRose and the reasons were...Pixie because of Faith, Trust and Pixie dust (Peter Pan one of my favourites) and the fact I love Tinkerbell and then it was either Rose after Dr Who or Belle after Princess Belle (one of my favourite Disney princesses) and Tink. Looking back PixieRose just seems weird. We rocked up to this big white house, but my poor baby was clearly being neglected (we think it was a farm. Adopt do not shop people). She snuggled into me immediately and slept in my arms the whole way home nuzzling on blankie (my first knitted project of which had holes and drop stitches all over it, but she loved/loves it) it was like she knew we were saving each other and that was it, PixieBelle was finally home.

Josh fell in love with her instantly, but she certainly did not! she wasn't keen on Danielle either really. Our other cats Teaser and Cloudy whom I had grown up with were not keen at first, but Teaser took her under her wing and taught her to hunt etc, Cloudy hated sharing me! Cats are so intelligent, when I would over exercise or Ana was too loud Teaser would either bite my ankles of nuzzle into my hair, when my heart was bad and I'd faint I'd wake up with her on my chest. Cloud would always come for hugs if I were upset, they were everything to me, when we lost them it broke me.

Anyway, PixieBelle was spoilt rotten (still is) and she really did her job as I was so distracted looking after her I didn't have time to let Ana in, she needed me and I knew that if I relapsed Mum would take P away. If there is one thing about Mum you should know it is that there are no empty threats, trust me on that! Later that month my first period came back and in all honesty I...was...MORTIFIED, what is a celebration for those around you that you're healing only reiterates that you're getting 'fatter' which is utter crap from Ana, it can come back whenever your body feels it can trust you enough to carry a baby should that be the case, isn't mother nature just incredible ? (I am serious, how cool!). A few days later however I felt the sense of pride and relief as all I want in life is to be a Mummy, so this was a huge positive and I eventually saw it this way. I saw my body trusting me, healing and allowing me to be a Mum one day.

At my next weigh in I had lost weight, but I was so defensive because I hadn't done it on purpose and as I cried to Mum terrified she would take P Mum chimed in over the ever cheerful K. 'Chloe, calm down. I read that you will lose after your period because we gain weight before, it's ok.' this is when Mum literally out educated K! It was **BRILLIANT**. At that point I felt so proud because not only was my body trusting me, but Mum was too! Mum even let me stay home for a few days when school restarted to look after P, and I ATE! I was now at a weight to start therapy because my 'brain was healthy enough to process', to this day I disagree with this theory, I think therapy should begin immediately because the process itself is torture ( I'm not sure if it has changed, I can only hope).

Sidenote, I was also working on my art A level at this time and I was doing it all on Anorexia, it was so therapeutic and Mrs S who was my teacher and organised it so I would get at least one A-level was incredible with me. My clay models were all based on Ana and it was just such a useful project for me, what is more is I passed.

My 18th birthday was in April and I had made it despite the whole 'she won't make it to her 18th (**HA UP YOURS K!**) why she was so negative who knows! I now had another form of therapy as well, hypnotherapy. Now, do not jump to conclusions here because it really was so helpful, one of my Instagram friends had recommended him. Ivan (my hypnotist) was so good, and I would come away with at least an hour or so of silence, I would be relaxed just that little bit. He was so optimistic and one of the first people to tell me to write a book that is, after Kirsty and Dad.

Unfortunately, Easter fell around my birthday as it always does and it was so difficult but this year, I wanted to be normal and so I managed some easter egg, I was so proud. I asked people that wanted to buy me an egg to scribble out calories or take it all out the box and put it in a bag and most of them did (someone covered it all in post-it notes, I can't remember who I think it was Amelie). I braved chocolate and although it took me weeks to eat in fact more than two months! I managed it, I was and still am a hoarder because in my distorted mind if I keep it then one day, I might be able to eat it.

The day arrived and I had a little cake, I was spoilt rotten and that evening we went to Bistro live (a club for these sort of celebrations) we ate a nice **THREE COURSE** meal (small portions) and I drank without worrying about calories, we danced on tables and I had a few moments where I felt very overwhelmed with emotions, I felt normal. The only normal bit I wish I could have skipped was throwing up! Josh unclipped my extensions and took my makeup off for me, we argued the next day and argued a bit on and off for a year about alcohol but as I explained, he had done his drinking underage bit and gotten s\*\*\*faced , I hadn't. I had not been a normal teenager and I was not going to be able to go clubbing alone for a while and that was not just because of Anorexia but Anxiety as well.

September 13th, 2015 one of my reasons to fight came into this world and to this day I am absolutely blessed and honoured to be her and her siblings 'Auntie Coco'! Ocean (Wednesdays sister) became one of my closest friends, I never would have thought that she would become one of my best friends considering before she got pregnant with Skylar-Blue she absolutely terrified me! (Love you!). Soon Kien-Luke would follow and then Hallie-Grace! Watching them grow up has been one of my reasons to stick around and keep fighting they have truly been a blessing.

### A mother's view:

Slowly weight was creeping on at a speed Chloe could just about handle. This was important because she could not mentally or physically handle too much too fast, it was dangerous in both ways. However, once she found PixieBelle she sped up a tiny bit and she gained 2.5lbs meaning she could, despite not being at the originally agreed weight she could get PixieBelle. February was upon us and a month into her new recovery she got her period back, I was over the moon (it is one of **CAMHS** highlighted 'recovery goals'). I had told Chloe that if she relapsed our hairdresser would take PixieBelle and if there's one thing about my parenting skills is that if I say I'm going to do something I will so Chloe knew I was serious, harsh …maybe but it's a necessary boundary.

April 4th, Chloe's 18th rolled around, and we had begun to get fed up with CAMHS' lack of hope. She had made it to 18, she was slowly winning just in her own time. Ivan was encouraging her every week (her hypnotherapist) and she knew in order to have a party out for her 18th she needed to eat. I was so enormously proud of her, we had a little cake and family around, she was spoilt by us all. We all knew how lucky and privileged we were that she had made it to this special day. AT the nightclub we danced on tables and had a normal party, I was sick not alcohol induced but emotion induced. I think I realised the enormity of how far we had come, and we were surrounded by those who had been through it with us. Chloe defied CAMHS' expectations again, we were getting good at that.

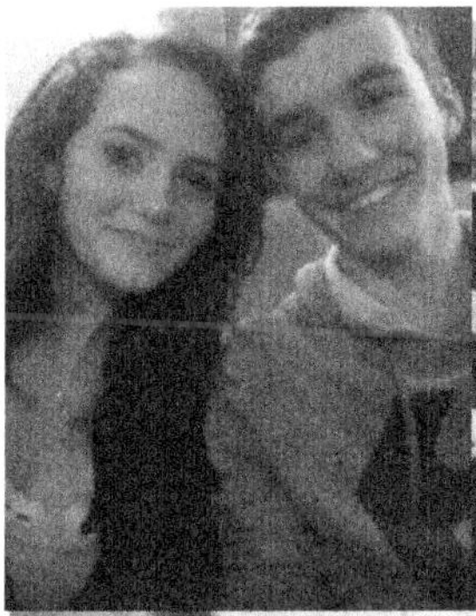
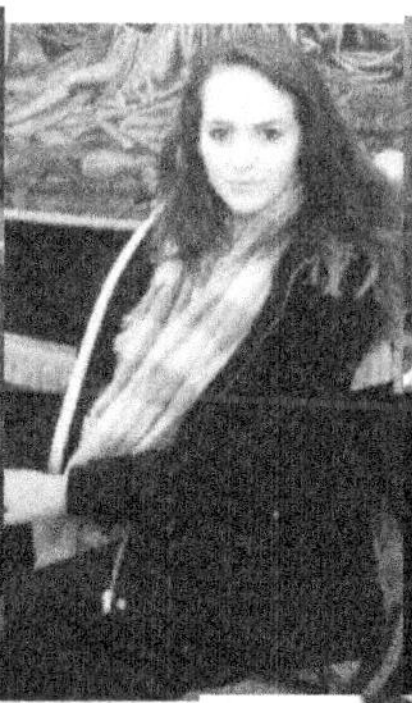
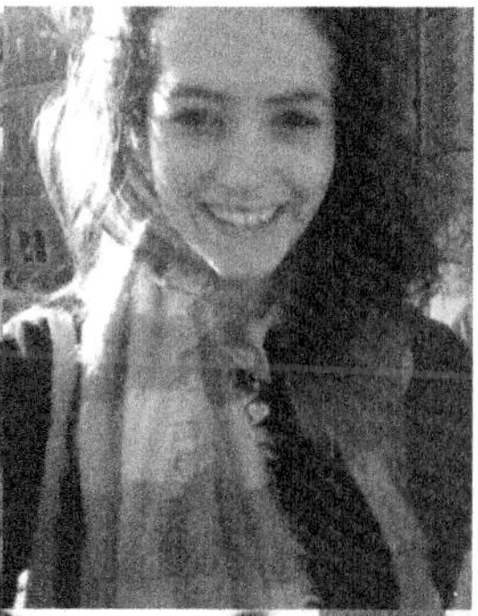
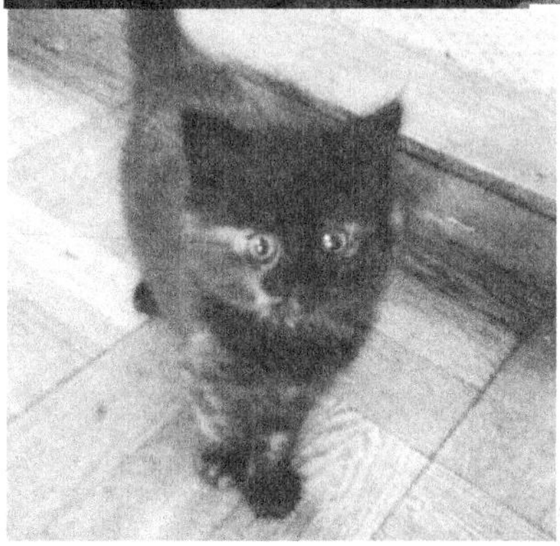
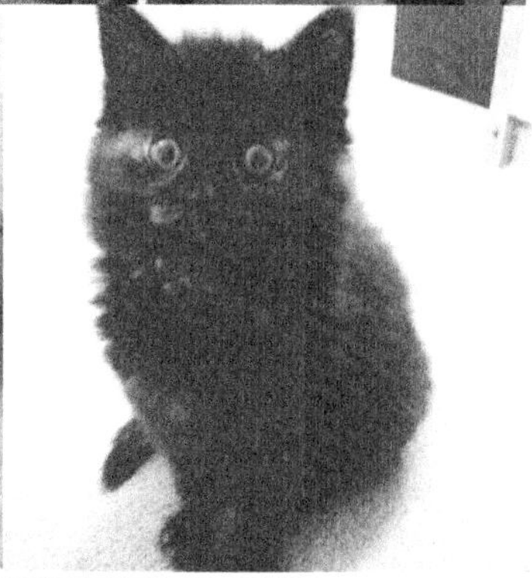
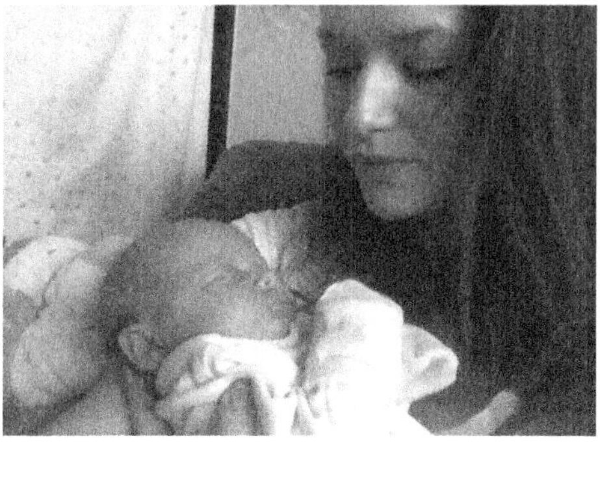

'The soul always knows what to do to heal itself. The challenge is to silence the mind.'

# Chapter Ten
## The C word.

Suddenly life was going well, I found myself competing in Miss Leicester and then the Miss England semi-finals. I met Kev Wise and he got me into modelling which I absolutely adore/d, I felt normal, I felt happy and then it happened. My world came crashing down.

In 2016 the battle switched to Mummy, she had pulled a muscle in her chest hoovering and she was worried about the lump as it was not going away. We assured her it was probably just a muscle and to get it checked out anyway but, out of me, Danielle and Daddy I was the only one who did not even allow the thought of cancer in. She went to the Drs and saw Dr Adcock and after assessing the lump he sent her to get a mammogram. When we arrived at the Glenfield, we were told they would scan and if they needed to biopsy, they would but I did not think for a second, they would. I was reassuring Mum and making her laugh etc (Ana was pretty much in the background by this point), and then they called her in, all I could do was sit, wait and hope to God that it would all be ok.

The man who would come and tell her she needed a biopsy was vile and I honestly wanted to punch him because he made her cry but alas I did not (lucky guy). Mum and I were then told the Dr would see us and I think Mum already knew at that point and my concerns were growing, there she told us 'I think it is cancer, It more than likely is and it's sitting behind your muscle so you're lucky you pulled it because we've caught it early'. I tried so hard to hold it together, but I broke and so the nurse looked at me and I said I need the toilet. I feel horrendous for leaving her in there and I do not think I will ever forgive myself, but I did not want to show weakness in front of her. The nurse (bless her) followed me and hugged me telling me it would be ok and that it was so early it would be a case of removing it and then chemo. The idea of My Mummy's red curls falling out broke me even more.

Anyway, I pulled myself together and went back in where I held Mummy's hand and took in all the information for her as she was (as most are) in a state of shock. Now it was my turn to repay the care that she gave me. I knew deep down it would be fine because as we have already established my Mum is a badass that no one messes with, not even cancer. I got home and left Mum and Dad a while to decompress as I went for a walk and tried to get hold of Josh, I couldn't so I tried Wednesday, again I couldn't get hold of her and so my best friend since 4+ was next and Laura was immediately calming me down. Wednesday rang back and then ran all the way from South Wigston to the church (our usual run to meet eachother in a crisis spot) and flung her arms around me. We chatted for a good hour and then I went home to the looming cloud of cancer. That thunder cloud of unknown hovering over us, Danielle had moved out by now and so she was told as well, and I believe she came over. The plan was we would go ahead with our Bulgaria holiday and then when we got home, she would have her operation. Dr Adcock and a few others were concerned I would slip back but I did not I held it together and damn am I proud of myself for that. I am not sure how Mum was so brave in Bulgaria and so normal, most of the time we did not think about it but when we did boy did it hit us. We went out to a big event near the end of the holiday and I drank... I drank a lot. This would become the first insight that something else was going on with me but at the time it was just a 'coping' mechanism.

When we returned home, they did the op and Mum was an absolute superhero! They wheeled her down, I held her hand the whole way until I could not go any further. I sat in the family room waiting for news and it seemed like a lifetime and then they said she was on her way up. On the way out of surgery she was already bolt upright in her bed telling me to go and get some food! She was also the nurse's pain of a patient on the ward as she refused to let me leave and I had to talk her into sleeping before I took her home! My Uncle Mark and cousin Finley had come to stay and had gone out with Danielle whilst we were sorting out the lump yet the next few days Mum was back on her feet she even came with us to Drayton Manor !! (bag holding obviously, that is, apart from her beloved carousel) I swear this woman is invincible.

Chemo started in September and would last for six courses, she had FEC-T which were told would be gruelling more so than some others. I dropped my Open Uni course and became Mums version of her!! I will never forget how hard that first session was, she tried the cold cap and it was gruelling, when we came home the numpty had orange juice even though she'd told us constantly as kids not to have it if we felt sick because it'd make us sick and yes indeed she was sick ! She went to sleep whilst I made shepherd's pie for us all.

We thought the cap had worked, but just a week before the next session the hair began to fall, I did my best to style it but this time I had to be harsh ' Mummy you're better of shaving it, it's making you more and more depressed, it's breaking you '. I hated myself for saying it because I could not imagine Mum without her red curls, I also felt very harsh. I left the thought with her and eventually we contacted Lisa (Dean's cousin) who had been amazing with getting my hair back to health and she came over as our friend to shave it. We giggle about the fact that after that people commented 'you have a really nice, shaped head'! I will admit I was very choked up as the hair fell to the floor and I scooped up a tiny bit to keep (I still have it). Picking out a wig was a long process and we thought she would go with something new, but she went to the same colour just straight!

Radiotherapy was next and then she had done it, my Mum had beaten breast cancer and now in 2020 she is four years clear and has done the mud run and given a progress canvas of hair loss and growth to the ward so that people can see it does come back. One thing I pride myself on is my response to a nurse's comment that 'if it's curly it comes back straight and vice versa'. My response 'no amount of chemo will take the curl out of that hair' ... I was right and now I am back to looking for the red curls in the supermarket when she wanders off!

**A mother's journey:**

I was diagnosed in July 2016 and now the battle was my own against breast cancer. I had my lumpectomy in August and Chemotherapy started in September, six courses every three weeks and then a month of radiotherapy. Wow, we really did not see that coming. But, somehow, Chloe could take care of me, somehow, she put her illness on the back burner, needing to be strong for me.

She came to nearly all of my Chemotherapy sessions and the only reason she didn't do all of them was because Danielle and my best friend Anita wanted to do their part. She would cook me dinner as I rested afterwards (admittedly she can make shepherd's pie better than me now!), she was amazing. All of my family were, they were strong for me, but they had great partners who were their shoulders to cry on.

So, 2020, I am 4 years in remission and my hair is finally growing back! Chloe continued to thrive.

'God, grant me the serenity to accept the things I cannot change; courage to change the things that I can: and the wisdom to know the difference.'

# Chapter Eleven
# Pixie's Project.

In late 2016, I was approached by Leicester Theatre Group and Charley Benns (Naked company). I had been a member of LTG prior to getting to sick and absolutely loved it. Every show, every rehearsal and the friends I made, honestly this place became my second home for about two years. Karl had remembered my illness very well, the last show I did was CATS and my knee was dislocating the majority of the time, I was having dizzy spells regularly and my weight drop was rapid. Karl, Hannah and Nikki picked up that there was something wrong way before my dance school which I always thought was strange because I'd been at dancing since I was 4 and these amazing people had only recently gotten to know me but nevertheless they were so supportive.

Karl and Charley asked if I would be happy to be involved in a project in which would educate others about Anorexia. I agreed and to my surprise the show would be based on MY journey and so work on Pixie's Project began, I was honoured to have been asked. I loved being so involved in the project from helping to select music to even casting the show; the girl who played me put her entire soul into it, all the girls did. I was so honoured that they wanted to tell my story and they wanted me to be a part of the whole process. Overall, we cast: Me, Wednesday, Josh, Mum, Danielle, Auntie Rachel, friends, Ana and her "friends".

Wednesday and I decided in order for the girls to fully understand our relationship and the stage of my illness we were trying to get them to depict we would have to re-enact one of the most painful moments in our friendship. We lay ourselves out for the scene in which she had tried to force feed me in France, there were tears on both our side and for those watching, we had a big hug after and I apologised once again. We would come to demonstrate a few more pivotal moments for us and in a way, I think it gave us both some therapy as we could resurface it but know that things were better now and that we made it. However, it caused a lot of discomfort, in both us and for the girls but it worked, and the girls aced it completely.

As well as the medium of dance to show the journey we also added dialect between Ana and myself. I wrote letters for G (OUR Ana) to read; in order to write them I sat in the other room notebook and pen in hand and wrote everything Anorexia was saying or had said to me. Sophie, who played me was incredible, she had curls just like mine (before I fried it with straighteners), and she worked so hard she actually ended up with blistered and scraped skin on her feet by the end of the show! I cannot thank the girls enough for how much work they put into it. We had Mum and Josh come in as well as Wednesday and they gave their views on what it was like for them, what they saw happen to me as a person as well as answering questions.

What was important to me was showing my Auntie Rachel as a guardian angel lifting me up showing the moment, I decided enough was enough. I also found some serenity in writing to myself for the end of the performance. Georgia (our Ana) was so incredible and was so spot on, when in character she made my blood boil which was a sign she was doing a good job. Amina who played Wednesday was unbelievably good at showing the emotions Wednesday felt, honestly, I had never been so proud.

Danielle did a photoshoot with the girls for the flyers etc and it was incredible, she did such an amazing job. I think there will always be some element of guilt around the projects casting as the girl originally cast as Ana ended up developing or already had Anorexia. I chatted with her mum and one of my friends who was her sister about it and eventually she got better but we did have to re-cast.

Beat, the UK's Eating Disorder Charity, sponsored the show and although there were only two performances it was a huge success. The idea was that we would tour but somewhere along the line things moved on without any planning to do so which was a shame. Instead, I told my story in other ways, spreading awareness and talking about my journey as well as offering support in schools and online. Initially, I began to tell my story in the media: magazines, newspapers, radio and even the Victoria Derbyshire show! Radio Leicester have had me in a fair few time and have always been amazing with me. The first time I went to Radio Leicester was before Miss Leicester and then I got to experience it again with Pixie's Project with Charley and again after that!

Miss Leicester was a huge moment in my recovery, firstly the work you put into the prep was just so rewarding. Fundraising is something I have always loved doing so I put on differently little events to try and raise as much as I could. Standing on a stage and walking that catwalk was amazing! I got that buzz I wanted, I felt so strong and empowered in my beautiful dress, hair and makeup done and just feeling like the old performing me again.

I was ambivalent about sharing my story as I know that the media likes to use skeletal images and numbers to sell the papers, but I was desperate to help people. Luckily, the journalists I worked with were/are amazing and let me write something to go alongside the images as a way of telling people that just because that's how I looked doesn't mean that's what they should strive towards or that they need to look like that.

Alongside the media, I created 'Pixies Project Organisation' my own charity/organisation in which I visit schools to tell my story, warn and offer advice as well as answering questions about my illness. I feel that in order for people to understand, for the stigmas to end, people need to be able to ask questions and so I have always been an open book about it. Pixie's Project does not disclose numbers of any sort and does not show any body checks as I believe this can trigger or even feed others.

Telling my story has been my priority throughout my battle with Anorexia Nervosa, I was inspired to speak out by, you guessed it... Demi Lovato. I wish someone would have told me their journey to show it gets better as well as telling others what they can expect in recovery, showing others that it is possible and what they are feeling is normal. I will forever be grateful for having the chance to see my own story live on stage, I didn't cry often at rehearsals, but at that final show I did cry, it's like something hit me and I was no longer involved in the production of just a 'show' I was involved in the production of my own story. This was my life, my story, live on stage in front of me, it was definitely surreal ,but also very cathartic. There have been the odd people, old friends who have disagreed with me speaking out, but I am proud of my journey and of the people I have helped.

When the show ended, we all went back to mine for an afterparty, I even had Pizza and we chilled out in the hot tub. The girls definitely needed hot tub time! Perhaps my favourite but also most insecure and vulnerable time was my letter to my body , watching the version of me stare towards her shadow and listen to my voice read the letter both broke me and also gave me the biggest sense of accomplishment and I truly wish I could feel that pride all the time.

So, I guess here is where I will put the letter...

'Dear body, I want to thank you. Thank you for being such a wonderful creation, thank you for fixing me and staying alive when the odds were so much against you. You could have crumbled, you could have given in, but you chose to keep me alive and for that I am so grateful. Thank you for dealing with my 'moments', I know I have hurt you in the past. I have abused and neglected you and for that I am so sorry. I was too naïve to believe that not eating would solve my problems, I am sorry for your ice-cold feet, I am sorry I made you work so hard and keep our heart beating. I am sorry for the laxatives and for only fuelling you with so little calories, I am sorry I took your teens, I'm sorry I shrunk you to such a vulnerable weight and suffocated you, I am sorry.

I am sorry for the cuts, burns, bruises and scratches and I promise you make it up to you every day. I'm sorry that I still compare you to everyone else when you have done so much to keep me alive. I am sorry for forcing you to be something you were not meant to be and for not caring for you as you have cared for me through the years.

I promise it will all be different now , I promise to care for you for as long as you'll let me .I promise no more scars and no more tears shed because you aren't what I think we should be. No more frustrated punches or pinching our skin so hard it bleeds and bruises. I know now that it's ok to have curves and it's ok to be warm. I'm sorry I denied you the nutrition you needed and I promise to fuel you as much as possible, I promise to never make you exercise to the point of collapse ever again. I promise no more ice-cold baths or weird fetishes to lose weight (like the green tea concoction... gross!).

I'm sorry for the sleepless nights, the stress and the pain. I'm sorry I didn't listen to the signs you were screaming, I'm sorry I played Russian roulette with our life. Most of all, I'm sorry I let Ana ruin us, you kept that little heart beating through the very worst and even then, you fought on.

Thankyou. Thank you for being you, thank you for growing and making me who I am, I promise to see our imperfections as perfections, as things that make me unique from now on. I will try to do you proud as you have done me. Thank you for the freckles, the curls I tried so hard to straighten, for the brown eyes that show my smile. Thank you for the pale skin (yes, I know... no more bad fake tans). Thanks for the curves, for the health you are trying to bring back, for the weird toes and for just being you/us.

I'm sorry I put you in survival mode, I'm sorry that you couldn't trust me and I pray one day you will and we will be in harmony with one another. Thanks for standing up when I tried to tear us down. Thank you for the tears you have wept and the smiles you've shone. Thank you for being **MY** body.

Thankyou for bringing me on this journey and our journey is far from over. We have such a life ahead of us now. I'm proud to call you **MINE**, yes, I may have my down days but know that I love you really. Yes, I will still more than likely straighten those curls and wear make-up but that's ok because there'll be days where I let the curls down and forget about the makeup. Thankyou body... for everything.'

Pixie's project is around when things started to turn mentally for me, I began relying on my Anorexia again to cope with other issues I was having , I was having urinary retention a lot which as a 19/20 year old wearing a catheter is not exactly my idea of fun. This I was told was a result of water loading and restricting to dehydration, I was also getting a lot of knee dislocations and palpitations. Something else was going on but we didn't know what, I was modelling with Kev Wise which gave me some confidence but something inside was hectic, something was stirring.

Matt, one of my closest college friends came to opening night alongside Wednesday (obviously), so many people supported it and I was so honoured, I still am to this day. The show was early 2017 and in March we lost our eldest cat Teaser, this hit me and made things tough, I didn't know life without her as she was there since I was born. Following this we lost Cloudy just two months later which broke me.

**A mother's point of view:**

My daughter surprises me even to this very day, with her bravery, confidence (yes, she does have this regarding talking about her illness) and courage to always try and help other people suffering from this awful illness. She truly is lovely through and through. She shows great empathy, even in her darkest times, and there have been a few unfortunately. Pixies project is one of the most positive and courageous things to come out of all this. It takes a brave individual to stand up in front of others and talk about a deadly disease that nearly killed her and was a traumatic time in her life. After the show there was a Q&A time, and I was so immensely proud of her as she stood there bearing her heart to strangers.

I hope Pixies Project will continue to thrive and the more people she can educate the better.

I have seen the magazine articles and again so enormously proud, but to this day, I cannot bring myself to look at those photos, at her poorliest. it breaks my heart; how could I have missed this? when it was happening right in front of my very eyes?

I have had a few interviews myself and I feel there is not enough information out there for us parents. a few leaflets here and there. Once I had watched Pixies project, I felt I understood the illness a little better.

However, there were many, many battles ahead where I would cry myself to sleep in frustration and concern.

### A best friend's point of view:

Pixie's project was hard for the fact that we had to relive a lot of trauma but in a way, we saw it as a way to heal, I think. The girls were amazing, and I was proud of Chloe for opening herself up so much but to start off with I was worried it would drag it all back up, I was worried she was taking on too much but then I saw how much it impacted her and made her see things differently and see things from my point of view.

I loved it and loved so much that I got to be a part of it. It really highlighted how our friendship had grown as she moved away from Ana and how we were still able to communicate and work together even though I had moved away to Hull.

### A boyfriend's point of view:

When Chloe first told me about Pixie's Project, I was extremely supportive of her and knew she could do it and I have always been supportive of her endeavours. I've never really understood interpretive dance but it was a really good outlet for Chloe, I think her creation of Pixie's Project Organisation and delivering seminars in schools about the disease is the best thing she has done in terms of eating disorders as it has had a direct influence on young people who may have been too afraid to reach out for help or unaware of what was happening to them.

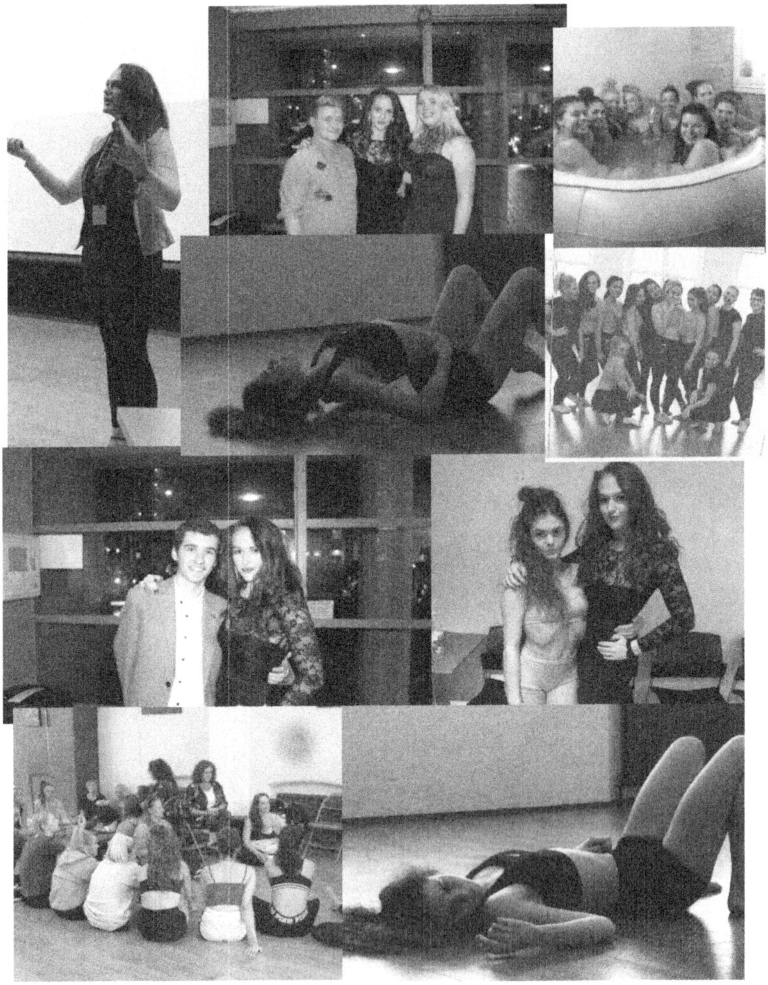

'Love is louder than the pressure to be perfect'
- Demi Lovato.

# Chapter Twelve
## Something isn't right here.

My depression suddenly went from intense to severe and I was upped to three fluoxetine tablets instead of two by Dr Adcock (this man is a saint for putting up with me). I was suicidal and Crisis team had no effect on me at all: in fact, they made things worse for me. I only deteriorated further and then in September 2017 I was sent to the crisis house for my depression.

Crisis house was a terrifying thought, and it was the closest thing to inpatient for mental health that I ever experienced. I remember agreeing to go because I did not feel safe, I was in A&E regularly for suicidal thoughts and it was taking over my life entirely, everything I saw I thought of a way it could hurt me. I remember packing and I was so worked up because we had just gotten Twinkle our new kitten and I didn't want to miss out on time with her, but I knew this would be the only place that could keep me safe.

When I got there all I wanted was PixieBelle and my family and josh, this huge room with an everlasting ceiling made me feel so small. I unpacked my things and tried to settle in (I would eventually but I am a home bird, so this was hard). Within days I picked up, I engaged in my therapy at 'Box Tree' (the facility) and I will always remember my room 'chestnut room', I just kept getting happier and happier, busier and busier so they took away my three anti-depressants and my mood continued to increase. I left crisis house on a high... literally.

A few weeks later I was in A&E again, this time believing I was an angel who knew when demons were around, I was admitted overnight, and they gave me a sedative because I hadn't been sleeping. Dr Adcock sent a referral to Cedars which was the psychiatrist near me, they are for other mental health issues instead of the ED service. The first Psych I saw was not great, I met with her in October 2017 and she left without telling me in January 2018 and she did not try to know me at all. I was first sent to a meeting by the previous psych for EUPD (emotionally unstable personality disorder) but whilst there I knew that was not what was wrong, the diagnosis just did not fit with me at all. As a result of her leaving I fell back on the wait list and it was not until August 2018 when things would change.

In August 2018 I experienced another high, Mum took me to wistow a garden centre in Leicester and all I was talking about was wanting a pet fish then two pet fish and it just kept going. I was not sleeping I had so much to do, I was talking so fast I don't think my mouth even knew how to catch up and my fashion changed significantly, and Mum just snapped. She had her suspicions on what was going on, but she did not assume, it had been discussed briefly in CAMHS but never again after that. A&E also had the same suspicion, but we had not had an answer... yet.

Enter Dr Anwar! Well where would I be without this amazing lady? I have never had a psych that can get around me so well or who knows me better than I know myself. She only had to meet with me twice to find out what was going on, Dr Anwar diagnosed me as Bipolar type 2. My diagnosis just made sense and I went to see her every 4 to 6 weeks depending, I started to stabilise on my Lamotrigine and then Dr Anwar decided it would be worth getting me a CPN to help with my care plan and that's where the wonderful Julie came in. Together the three of us worked on trying to stabilise my Depression and my Hypomania.

I think I always knew something was going on because I was not trying to control anything as far as I knew but I think it was always my moods I was trying to control without really knowing it. I think this became clear as my 21$^{st}$ year was the best year of my recovery. Dr Anwar was really understanding of all I was going through and still is, she sees me and not a patient's file and I think that is what makes her so unique. When I was high I experienced and still do experience some real unreasonable beliefs such as 'I'm special I don't need food' or I drink and take unnecessary risks, I often get the itch to pierce, tattoo or dye my hair and tend to not sleep as my list of creative tasks and overall pointless tasks grows beyond my control and the world just seems too slow as my thoughts dart and race. Depression really gets me, I cannot be bothered to fight with Ana, to do my makeup or even clean my teeth (gross I know), I can't bring myself to do anything but wish for death, fantasize about how life would be better without me in it, how I am a burden and how nobody likes me but alas I am getting ahead of myself.

Dr Anwar and Dr Adcock came together to keep me on track and I am so grateful to God for writing the old Dr out of my life because I honestly cannot imagine another Dr other than Dr Anwar looking after my mental health. Somehow, even when my brain wants me to keep secrets, she manages to get through and navigate my brain better than I can and I tend to come out of sessions when I am depressed, or Ana is bad a completely different person: regardless of the length of that normality.

Julie and I also built a really good relationship and between the three of them my care team was formed, and it was/is the dream team! Box Tree was a pivotal moment in my journey, if it was not for the therapy and the team there noticing something was wrong then I don't think I would've known for a long time. I remember bits of my hypomania but very little as I tend to block it out although the spending catches up with me!!!!

With my mental health I have this self-destruct habit and when things are going well it's like my brain has to self-destruct and Dr Anwar is very understanding of this. Whether it's self-harm, anorexia, drinking, taking risks or abusing pills: she just knows how to a)bring me back to earth and make me aware that I am self-destructing b) get through to me and c) get me back on track.

### A mother's point of view:

well crisis house was amazing. I felt when I dropped her off, I had failed Chloe. I had not managed to help her. but eventually I realised she needed the professional help these wonderful people could offer. while Chloe was in, I had the best sleep id had in an exceptionally long time. I remember feeling wonderful, then guilt! the brain is a complexed organ!

Her psychiatrist is amazing. for once, I could relax when she went there, as I knew she would feel 10 times better when she came home. only Dr Adcock had the same effect on her. it was great to think she had support and that, us as a family including Josh also had the support when we needed it too.

finally, people were able to understand Chloe as well as we did, and it has impacted positively on us all since then.

### A boyfriend's point of view:

Chloe had a tendency, to switch moods on and off in periods. Depression was never an 'oh that could be bipolar' it was always an 'oh that's the eating disorder or relapse' but when she got the diagnosis I was scared, I didn't know anyone who had Bipolar and the mania side was scary. The depressive side of Chloe is manageable, I can leave her be if she is moping and I can push her to do stuff but with the mania there is no getting through and it is so much harder and scarier to deal with.

When Chloe called herself a 'messenger of god' and was fixated on the 'government watching us' I started to realise there was definitely something wrong, something else was definitely going on. Dr Anwar clearly had a positive impact on Chloe's mental health and it was good to finally have someone reliable on the mental health side of Chloe's life as me and her family could emotionally support her and Dr Adcock was another positive influence and now we had Dr Anwar on board too.

'Why do I compare myself to everyone? And I always got my finger on the self-destruct?'
-Demi Lovato.

# Chapter Thirteen
## Make a wish.

Firstly, I find it ironic that this chapter happens to be my lucky number! So, April 2018 had come around at this point and I need to highlight that not only had I reached my 18th but now I had reached my 21st! So... cough, cough, CAMHS you suck, and you were wrong AGAIN!

I celebrated my 21st in style with a Demi Lovato inspired birthday cake and a party and I mean a PARTY! If there is one thing my family does well it is a party. The theme was rose gold and black and I had a positive motivational quote on every table. Wednesday had told me she could not come, and I was utterly heartbroken! I spent weeks praying that she would get time off work, but she did not. Skylar, my gorgeous fairy goddaughter came running in and I was so distracted that I did not notice that not only was Ocean there with Trev and the kids, but WEDNESDAY had surprised me. Well, needless to say, I cried... A LOT. I am still pretty surprised that Josh kept that a secret as he is rubbish at secrets! Skylar-Blue followed me around with her little balloon for most of the night and I was happy, I was comfortable and I was surrounded by those that I love, people who came from all over just to celebrate with me.

So, at this point my mental health was stable, sure I wobbled a bit here and there, I jumped to a few diets, but I was well. Josh and I were and in the best place and everyone was content, Anorexia was a thing of the past. Amelie was growing up fast and I was so thankful I was alive to see her grow, we had a little dance that night and my heart was so full. My cake was New York and Demi Lovato themed (my two favourite things) and yes, I even ate some. I gave a little speech thanking those who had travelled far and me and Eddy (Wednesday) had a dance to 'A Thousand Years' which is our song.

I managed to get Josh on the floor for a dance to our first dance song 'Thinking out loud'. However, despite Ana being a thing of the past for everyone else, I was still listening to her onslaught of abuse every day. Ana was in the back of my mind. I had hit a certain size on my jeans and it was killing me, I hated every second of it and I began to panic although I did hold on for dear life.

Why? Because on June 30th, 2018 I saw my hero Demi Lovato live in Birmingham. I had had an amazing 21st year so far, me and Josh had spent the 27th at Alton Towers and I honestly was so excited to see Demi I do not think I shut up all day. I missed out on meet and greet tickets which literally killed me, what else could be better than telling your hero she saved your life? but I sucked it up after the tears!!! So, let me just explain here, I have been a fan of Demi since day one and if it was not for her, I would not be alive. Demi was the reason I got help for Ana, her music the reason why I stayed alive, her quotes kept me going, her laugh made me smile and she really did save my life. In fact, Mum thought I had Bipolar after reading what Demi had said in an interview about her own journey.

I was so excited for the concert, what was more... I went with Wednesday, who was very tearful to be standing beside me, alive as she never thought we would make it.

Now I had a letter that I had poured my heart and soul into, telling Demi what she had inspired me to do and how she had kept me alive. I was determined would make it to Demi , albeit she was going through her own shit at this point so it probably never made it but I gave it to her bodyguard ( I recognised him but just saw the lanyard and thought 'he can get backstage, he can take my letter !). Steve, the bodyguard listened to my story about how Pixie's project was continuing because of Demi's strength and honesty. I explained how in my darkest moments Demi kept me alive. Without paying much attention I rambled on whilst he attached a label to my wrist giving us a pass to SIDE STAGE!!!!

I can remember her coming on stage as if it were yesterday. She looked beautiful and OH...MY...GOD was she incredible live!!! There, side stage, I screamed my lungs out and she HELD MY HAND. I cannot explain the excitement and honestly as much as I still want to meet my hero one day, that was enough at the time.

Demi was amazing and the whole time we were there Ana did not dare haunt me: I spent the whole night singing with my best friend and honestly at the end I cried my eyes out.

We stayed at a hotel in Birmingham and ordered room service, we had a few drinks but not a lot as we were more focussed on being in the moment. When we got back to the room (after me loitering around to see if we would see her) we flopped into bed and just had our usual long girly chat before calling it a night. I will never forget the whole experience, even getting lost trying to meet Wednesday at her coach station, I even did the train ALONE! a huge step for my anxiety.

We went to five guys the day after as we had to go our separate ways which did and always will kill me! I ate FAST FOOD and I walked round in my hundreds of pounds worth of Demi Merch and my bomber jacket that my Gran had made for me after I missed out on the official one. Ana was beginning to surface a little more and I was pushing her to the back of my mind as much as I could, but she was not backing off.

**A best friend's point of view:**

Do not get me started on Chloe's obsession with Demi Lovato, this girl has adored her for so long and I swear Demi could talk her round because by using Demi quotes and playing her songs I could calm her down. A song to stop the panic attacks, a hug and a quote to get her to eat, her fangirling saved her life to an extent.

The concert was everything and seeing Chlo so happy was everything to me and if you could have seen her face you would understand how much she fawns over this woman.

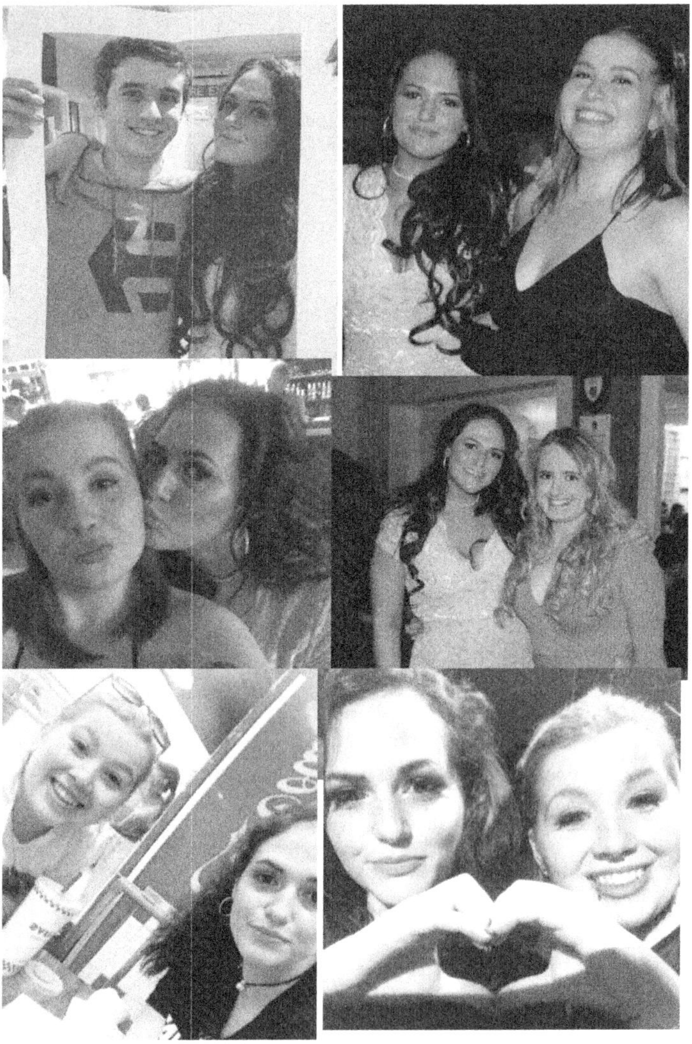

'Welcome to New York, It's been waiting for you,

welcome to New York,

welcome to New York.'

- Taylor Swift.

## Chapter Fourteen
## The City of Dreams.

Time, sometimes it seems like a whirlwind of days, hours and ever dragging minutes. Right now, in that moment in my memories, it is still... nothing could interrupt the cold wave of wind upon my face, the bright lights shining below me and the night sky allowing them to do so. I had imagined that moment every day of my life since I was five years old. I had pictured the lights in my darkest times and now exactly four years to the day of the most memorable and painful day of my life I had made it.

Four years from the day I decided that no one else could save me from this monster consuming me, but myself. She had taken every part of me, every breath, every smile and every part of my soul. She had pierced through me like a blade and slowly I had bled out, slowly I had lost those dreams. The five-year-old had begun to slip away, bleeding out of me as I lost every sense of who I was.

Where was I at that moment in time? four years from the day I fought back? New York City: I stood at what seemed like the top of the world, looking down at the skyscrapers below, feeling every single emotion possible, every sense heightened, I exploded with the pride inside. The freezing winds did not take away that moment, the drizzling rain brushing my skin and the hustle and bustle of the city below was like ecstasy to me. The creation of a memory, the five-year-old little girl inside my heart jumped in excitement. The memory of a dying girl granted me peace and wished me well as the memory of her passed on, the twenty-one-year old who had lived what seemed like a thousand lives stood proud, falling further in love with the city below her.

It was a far cry from the hell I had been through to get there, something inside of me pulled me up from the ashes of Anorexia's fire and granted me a second chance at life. Through all the blood, sweat and tears recovery provided, it was all worth it: every single minute since that night (the night I felt my body decaying beneath the iron fist that was Anorexia) I had clawed my way to every milestone and lived every second as though it was my last.

Right then, in that moment, the empire state building was no longer the dream that could never be reached, right there and then, it was my prize, my reward for fighting every single day; from fighting for every breath to breathe in this cold New York wind.

I stood with a full tummy of food from 'The Olive Garden', feet burning and bruised from all the walking, but I did not care, for me it was bliss. For me, they were a reminder that this was real. They had walked me to a thousand places but non-compared to this. For a moment my phone was not glued to my hand, instead it hung by my side as I became another New York dreamer that had reached their destination. I was merely a tourist whose story was not visible to those around me but to my mum and sister, I was a dreamer and the creator of a new life for myself, without her.

New York was the best, the night before we left there was a 4-hour gap to sleep in and whilst Mum and Danielle slept... you guessed it! I was up checking I had everything including my checklist of sites to see. I played my Taylor Swift and Demi Lovato albums the whole flight and I was so bloody happy that as the plane came into land 'Welcome to New York' played, it was like a film.

I ate foods I had only dreamt of, watching all the food shows and mukbangs on YouTube for years, dreaming of the day I would be brave enough to say 'yes' when offered food, the ability to order for myself without tremoring and changing my mind. We went to madame Tussauds whilst we waited for our spot at the Hard Rock Cafe which was AMAZING. I remember exactly what I had and what it tasted like but the thing is with Ana, she's always there even when you feel like you have won , she is always in the back 'you're going to end up so fat', 'let me take over , just for a bit, I'll make you happy and safe again'.

Unfortunately for her even through the guilt of food, I ATE!!! I left bits of most meals as the portions were MASSIVE but the one thing, I did finish was the French toast. It was the most amazing breakfast ever, we had a 'sandwich' before we took our flight back to England (it broke my heart). This sandwich was definitely NOT a sandwich, it was a burger, and it was enormous but really tasty.

I had THE BEST Pizza I had ever tasted; I'm not being dramatic here I swear. One day I hope I can go back and get the same pizza, warm pepperoni pizza whilst the city was freezing cold! I tried snow cones, pretzels (not a fan), Hershey hot chocolate, pasta at the olive garden and so much more. Including my 3 musketeers bar of which I purchased with my one dollar from Wednesday who four years before had returned with a dollar from her ski trip with the school. She had presented it to me and told me that one day, when I made it to New York I would have to use it to buy a chocolate bar. Wednesday never gave up on me, yes at the 'Tell me you love me' tour she was thankful I made it but deep down she knew I would.

We visited all the crucial places and although I never made it to Brooklyn, I swore one day I would. A part of me has always been obsessed with America, I do not know why but it has. Mum says she saw a change in me in New York and had a bad feeling, but we carried on as I thrived in a place that felt like home instantly. We did a lot of shopping and I bought a Tiffany bracelet with my birthday money, it was like a dream. I love 'Breakfast at Tiffany's' as well, so I recreated the Audrey Hepburn picture whilst there. Danielle trekked us all around the city to look for trainers for Dean and we did so much more shopping that by the end of the trip I think my feet were ready to drop off. I went into all the VS stores I could find but a fair few times I looked at myself and thought 'what have you become you fat cow' alas my sister had me creasing in laughter the majority of the trip and we finally had that New York trip she and I had both wanted all those years ago.

Central park was gorgeous, and I embraced every gossip girl site possible. I was starting to look at photos here and see flaws, see chubby cheeks and boobs. I HATE BOOBS. I think I hate boobs because they're known to be a product of fat and that stresses me but also mainly because mine started at a C then when I got sick they shrunk to AA and now back up they look like deflated balloons and I feel fatter with them. Despite her nagging she did not interfere with my dream holiday and what was the cherry on the top was the Christmas shops!! Although the amount of times Mum dragged us in, me and Danielle started to tease her.

The amount of walking compensated for the thoughts and I was just so overwhelmed with the city and the joy that she just did not affect me at all. We visited the Statue of Liberty where I had the most amazing Crab sandwich ever. I cried as the plane left, who would've thought that the sick emaciated girl would not only make Christmas and New Year, but she would reach her 18$^{th}$ AND her 21$^{st}$. There's still so much I have left to do in New York and hopefully one day I can go back, perhaps even finish a meal. I have definitely left a part of me in New York.

## A mothers point of view:

NYC... somewhere I was not really bothered about going to. but when you have Chloe banging on and on about it constantly! myself and Danielle decided we could do it. The men went skiing in January, so we nipped into the Coop travel and booked her dream trip! well that was it, the start to a VERY long countdown! it was an amazing trip. I really enjoyed it. I was surprised by how much I did. there is just something about the city that captures you and lets you dream.

We loved it. but most of all, I loved spending time with my girls. we have such a special relationship and we have so many laughs when we get together. we laughed at all the places Chloe dragged us to. However, I was worried, she would hit rock bottom when we went home. you know how it is? you look forward to something for so long, then it is gone. you are lost. just like Christmas! she was always like that as a child, she would start to get excited for Christmas in October, and the January would arrive and down she would go. you can see why i was concerned. I knew she was covering up how much Ana was taking over again. i was concerned we did not have anything to hold over her, to keep her striving to recover. We had fulfilled all her dreams, we had to go back to the drawing board to think of another reason for Chloe to stay alive. It was a constant battle to keep her positive and not let Ana convince her she was the best option. this can get very tiring, but we all get on with it, what is the alternative? not a thought I ever liked to think about. we were all on the same page, no way was Chloe going down that road again....

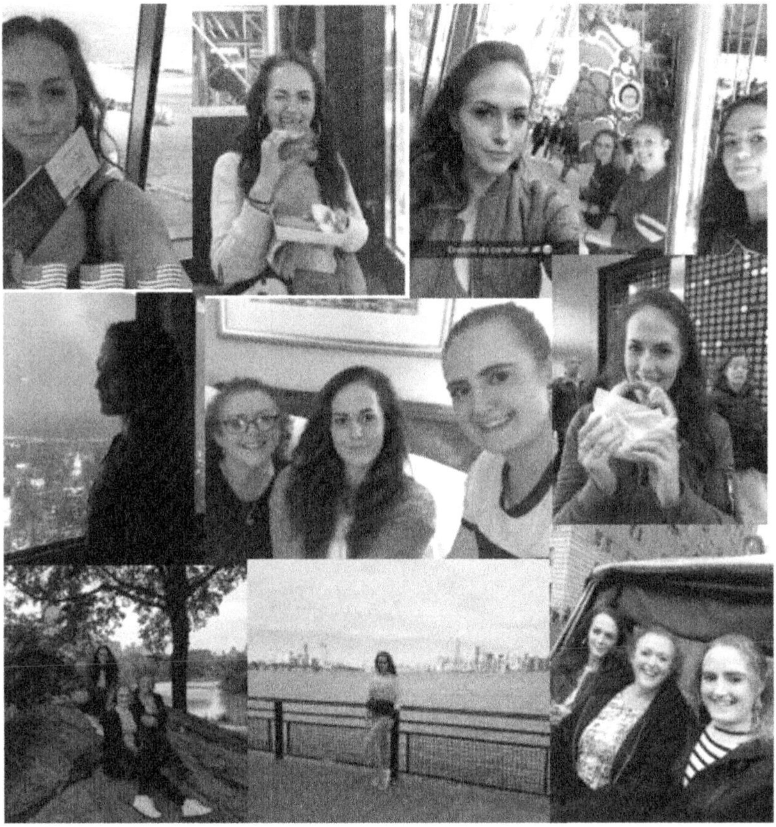

'You have this unquenchable need to self-destruct.'
- Orange is the new black

# Chapter Fifteen
## Something snapped.

There is a part of you that just clicks, just like a light switch. It is that quick, one minute you are ok and the next, it's all gone. All the work you did you no longer care about. Nothing matters anymore, the entire function of your day, everything you do depends on what she wants you to do next. No matter what you do you are never good enough. It happened in Christmas 2018 right before things took a turn, I was taking a lot of photos and there it was... the fat, the roll the lump. I felt such guilt, such hatred and I suddenly felt like I was drowning but I did not want to stop.

At the end of the day, letting her back in is not a choice, it is overwhelming. It is not just a case of ignoring it and it will go away. It is pulling for freedom from her claws but then running back to her for comfort and safety. The problem was that by letting her in was ultimately shutting the doors on everyone who loved and cared about me. I did not feel like I deserved love, I was fat, disgusting and unworthy of affection. Josh was merely with me out of courtesy, right? Wednesday would hate me, and I would lose her, right? Mummy and Daddy would walk away, right? WRONG...WRONG AND WRONG. Yet I isolated myself from the world, locked myself inside the cage and let Ana take over, I refused to admit I was in over my head.

**January 2019.**

I began to restrict towards the end of January. Slowly but surely my portions of dinner shrunk, and I was skipping as many meals as I could, laxatives came back briefly but instead I just stopped eating. Hunger makes you feel a few ways but for me I get a high. I feel like I am floating above the world but then it hits me after a few weeks, the overwhelming sense of exhaustion and pain. Following this...I decide to eat, I never binged, I simply have breakfast, lunch and dinner all remaining at a certain restriction but just enough to give me some umph. The overwhelming guilt that follows makes me regret every bite that I have taken. The disobeying of your disorder causes a hatred deep into the pit of your stomach and you wonder why you bothered anyway. For me it becomes a project, an incessant need to achieve the best I can, I am a perfectionist so once I start, I cannot stop without this sense of failure.

I convince myself that I will wake up with fat clinging to my bones if I eat, how silly is that to normal people? But to me and a lot of other Anorexics and probably other sufferers of eating disorders to, there's this utter fear that when we eat it will make us gain weight overnight and yes whilst it will add weight of the food, once it passes through your system, your weight does not change. From my own research it takes an awful lot to make you gain at least a pound of permanent weight overnight.

**February 2019.**

I went to see a nurse in 2019 for some blood tests and I broke down in tears, I told her I was losing weight and that I was restricting and could not stop. She went next door to Dr Adcock who saw me immediately and arranged to see me every two weeks to keep an eye on me, but it did not stop me.

I was nannying a second family at this point and the stress of the environment compared to nannying the boys that I nannied/y fed the disorder. I was also fed up with not being able to exercise because of my knee and its persistent dislocations (I have had bad knees for a long time due to hypermobility). On my way to work I pulled over (early as usual) and for a minute I felt like life was heading in the right direction, like I was fighting again. Yet I felt plagued , I sat listening to 'sober' by Demi Lovato (a song I would sing at open mic at our local a few weeks later which in a way was a cry for help) and I reminded myself on that cold winter morning that my soul would not become as dark and empty as the sky in front of me, my eyes will not fall into that hollow pit again. I will not give in I thought to myself, I will keep trying and one day ... maybe soon, maybe not but with every fibre of my being I was craving to be free.

Perhaps this time it will be different? Perhaps this time I will stop when it is time? Perhaps I will know when to stop? 'NO' I screamed at myself abruptly in the car (if there was anyone awake passing by I would definitely look like I was crazy... crazier), 'no Chloe' she is toxic, she always will be, she is a parasite. Alas, a few weeks later I found myself ice cold, tears dripping down my face as I sat in the car yet again, the pain writhing inside, and it becomes nothing but a void.

<u>March 2019.</u>

I had a Pixie's Project talk and by this point a lot of people had started to catch on. Mum says she had her suspicions but was waiting for me to speak up and Jon (Josh's dad) was one of the first to notice (bless him, honestly love my second family so much). My friend Alanis had convinced me to tell Wednesday and it didn't go overly well, I got the silent treatment for a while and I told Ocean who was really supportive often using the kids to get me to eat ( I can't say no to my fairy godbabies).

At the Pixie talk I was honest and told them I was relapsing, by this point I had a letter from Dr Anwar (review of each appointment) in which 'in remission' had been removed from the diagnosis bit and instead it just read 'anorexia nervosa'... that killed me. I refused to go back to eating disorder service as they only made me worse and Dr Anwar, Dr Adcock and Julie were a thousand times better even though they all always tell me they don't know how to go about it, they've done more for me than ED services ever did.

Dr Anwar was amazing with my ambivalence and told me it 'wasn't necessarily a bad thing, it means you've not given up on the possibility of getting better'. That has always stuck with me and in fact I have it printed and laminated on a piece of paper to remind me along with 'resilience comes from adversity'. March 20th came around and I sat across from perhaps, in my opinion at least, the best psychiatrist in England, the woman who fixed me and understood me faster than anyone else before her. She discussed with me that I could either tell my family now and them be on my side or continue to lie to them and in 6 months' time where would I be.

Each time she suggested something Ana turned it around and I found myself saying 'but' every time Dr Anwar came up with an idea. I know she is right, and I knew she had a point with each word she said she rattled Ana's cage because she is one of very few who can get through to the real Chloe. I remember her face when I told her 'if I get low enough then my recovery weight won't be as high' and 'just a little while longer and then I promise ' she probably wanted to shake me at this point. She told me that Josh and Mum would notice eventually, and she looked at my weight sent by Dr Adcock and I knew she was worried. I have this need to please people and if I like that person, I will try extra hard, so I felt like I was letting them down. I was told that perhaps it would be better if they found out from me because then I would 'still have control' which was so unbelievably right and definitely helped. I have never had a psych who cared/s about me as much as she did/does, likewise with Dr Adcock, their hearts and souls are in their work and that is what makes them so incredible. I wanted to make them proud.

Dr Anwar tells me that it is not a black and white situation it is a sliding scale and just because I messed up does not mean I have to call myself a failure. I said to myself 'that's it, I quit' I bought a special spoon to encourage eating that said 'to live would be and awfully big adventure' and I prep myself and then, there it was, on the scale, down again and now I was clawing for survival.

I remember the moment before I told them, where I came home sat down on the sofa and just cried saying to Mummy and Daddy 'I'm not ok, I've relapsed', I thought they would be furious but instead my Daddy held me as Mum told me she knew and had suspected for a while, but wanted me to admit it instead of accusing me or provoking Ana.

Josh, however, was not so understanding. We had a huge blow out and he just didn't understand, I got so worked up and my parents had to explain to him that it wasn't me lying but Ana. It is really hard for people to understand the difference between an eating disorder and the individual. Anorexia can make you a completely different person, I cannot lie to save my life, but Ana can make me a liar, a thief, a manipulator and a stone-cold bitch.

<u>April 2019.</u>
Well, I would be ringing in my $22^{nd}$ year hating myself once again for what I had done and what I had failed to do. Snap, the camera captures a selfie, I take it because I want to see how fat my face is from a weekend of birthday celebrations. I had begun bodychecking a week before my birthday and at this point, I was in maybe the 30s or 40s with how many photos I had taken. I looked at the selfie and saw eyes of pain and emptiness, trapped once again. The body checks came as I tried to eat again, I took them regularly but at swimming I did not like what I saw. I saw a body in pain screaming out for nutrients, yeah sure the bones gave Ana satisfaction but then she was screaming 'fat' again only seconds later. Following this I began counting my calories again watching YouTube videos of people eating what I wish I could eat. I watched what models ate (fyi my anorexia has never been fuelled by models unlike the stereotype) they showed me I didn't need to starve that they ate three meals and snacks a day with exercise and healthy fats.

<u>May 2019.</u>

Anorexia makes you feel this unimaginable amount of grief and distress the second you defy your disorder you want to run to it wanting its arms holding you tightly again because the thought of eating 1,000 is too much. I had eaten over what was acceptable and I felt physically revolted and dirty. My brain hurt and I wanted nothing more than to curl up into a ball and never eat again. Would I run back to restriction? I was scared and uncomfortable, so I went back to what I knew... restriction.

Snap went the camera, swoosh as the tape measure unravelled. The numbers had moved the tiniest bit, and I had a meltdown, why did I let myself get this way again. Then it hit me, Ana was making me do this for fuel to her fire she wanted me to feel this way, to run into her arms. I was not even giving my body a chance in recovery.

I was losing Wednesday or at least that is what I thought but as we met again, she seemed shocked and infuriated towards Ana. She makes me eat chips with our cocktails and explains she didn't ignore me for any other reason but that her heart had sunk, and she thought I wouldn't survive this again. She was protecting herself; I was hurting her.

I walked into Dr Adcock for my appointment and he is always very honest with me. He told me 'you look worse' and 'I'm worried we have more to deal with here than we thought'. I explained that each time I left I wanted to change but within minutes she had roped me back in, he stated what we both knew was the truth as I begged for one more week before he would ring ED services which we had agreed but as I said it he replied ' 7 weeks now you have been saying the same thing Chloe... give me one more chance'. I managed to improve after this and so Ana had time to re-group, I guess.

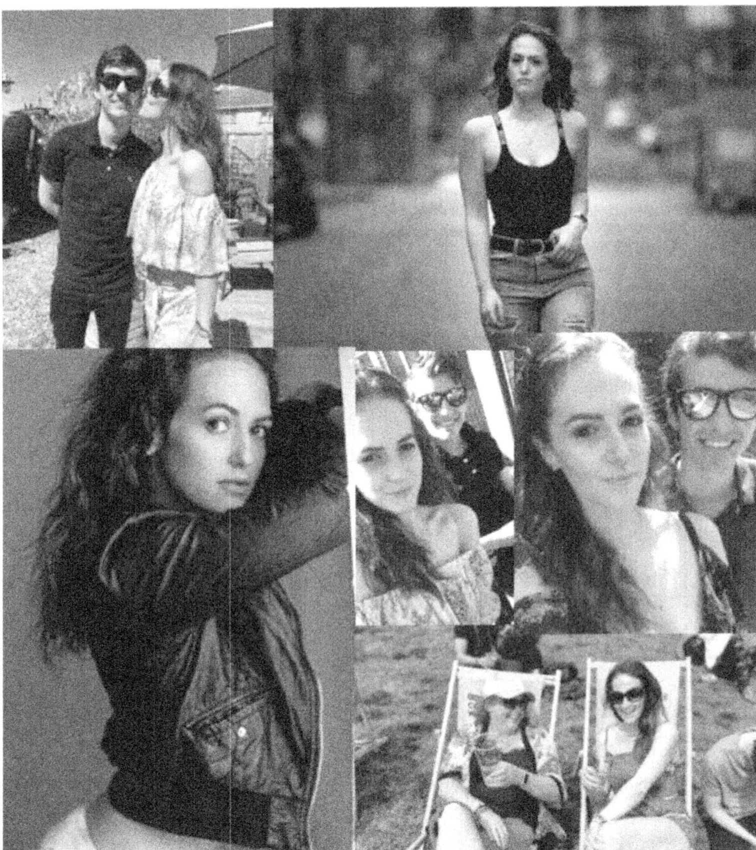

## July- August 2019.

We went to France in the summer and I was doing well yet again, there was a big group of us which me and Dr Anwar have decided is not the best environment for me as I always seek approval and want to be liked by everyone so I try too hard. Anyway, despite the last few days I had the most amazing time, and I don't think that I had really had a laugh in months until me and Danielle spent the summer together. Danielle and I both attempted to remember our French, we laughed about Mums hot flushes and D even calmed me down when I was triggered.

Danielle and Dean brought their dogs with them (Lola and Milo) and so I had plenty of cuddles and distractions with my fur-niece and nephew. We also had my Uncle and cousin which made the holiday so special. I ate and obviously ate my macarons because duh!

We went to chateaux's and shopping, threw eachother in the pool and visited all the local landmarks. I even braved some real fear foods. It was such a lovely time, and I did not mind how my body looked at all.

Things were going well but then we came home, and it was time for round two. Ana was not letting go without a fight.

## August 2019.

Luckily, I had what my psychiatrist called the 'dream team', this would keep me out of ED services which at this point was in my best interest. Our dream team consisted of me, Dr Anwar, Dr Adcock and Julie. Dr Adcock had done this with me so many times, but I could tell he was worried and disappointed, it killed me because I wanted to make them proud. He would continue to weigh me and monitor my bloods and I had to agree to this and follow through after all it was in my best interest. I would attempt to up my intake whilst Dr Anwar monitored my mental state.

They were/are my lifeline, I was aching with guilt for hurting those around me, for putting them through this again, ah guilt... the feeder to Anorexia's games. 'Anorexia isn't something that goes away Chlo, it is a thing of remission, it will always be there' Dr Anwar said and she was right I just had to find some fight but the thing was at this point I didn't care anymore. I did not care about the dropping numbers or the bad blood results, in fact at this point I was ready to die.

The thing is ... no one tells you about the sick wanting for protruding bones and the yearning for that faint feeling to tell you, you are doing what is 'right'. No one can imagine the pit of darkness and the guilt that comes with this illness the knowing that regardless of those around you, you are completely on your own. As things worsened, I debated speaking up, I debated it, but she just would not let me. I had an impending weigh in, and I was terrified but also thankful that someone was monitoring me.

August 31ˢᵗ I met my second beautiful fairy goddaughter Hallie-Grace and all I could think was this was how it went last time, last time I was sick I held Skylar-Blue as I started to fight and now I was doing the same with Hallie. I watched Kien playing and how gentle he was being with Hallie, I saw Skylar look at her adoringly and all I wanted was to watch them grow up, to have my own children and see them grow up, I did not want Ana, I wanted a future.

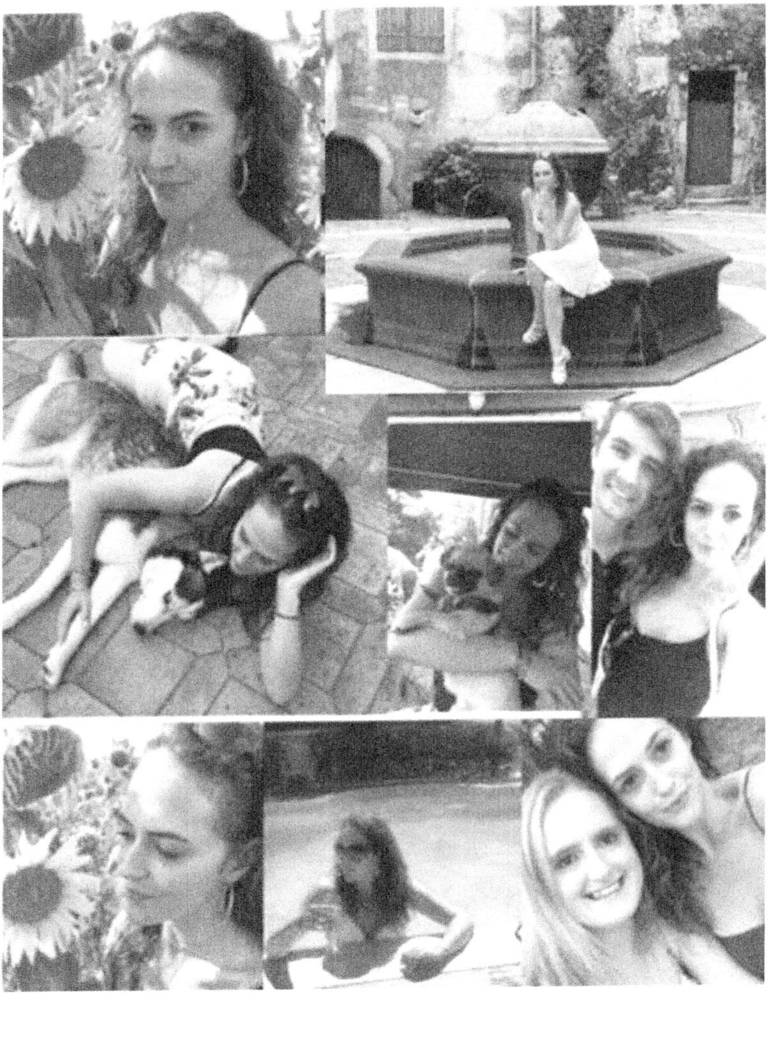

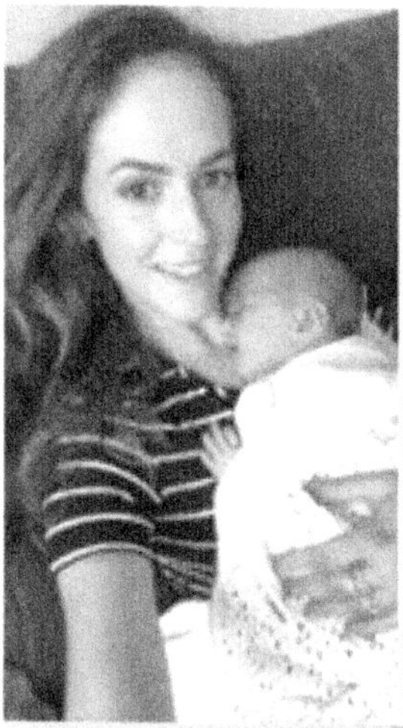
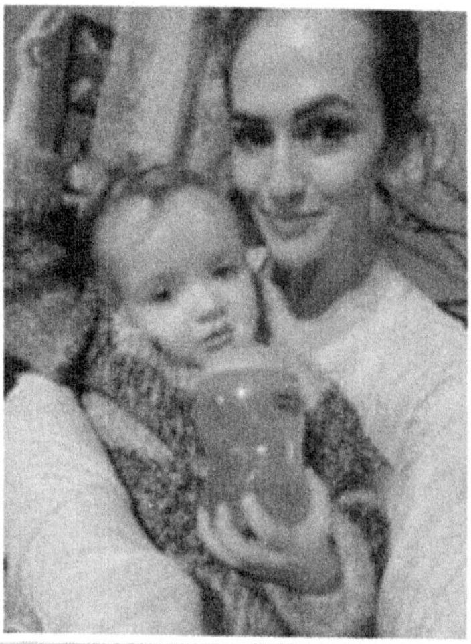
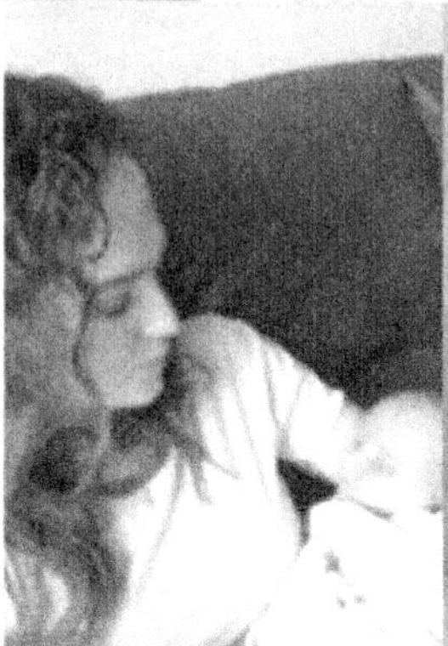
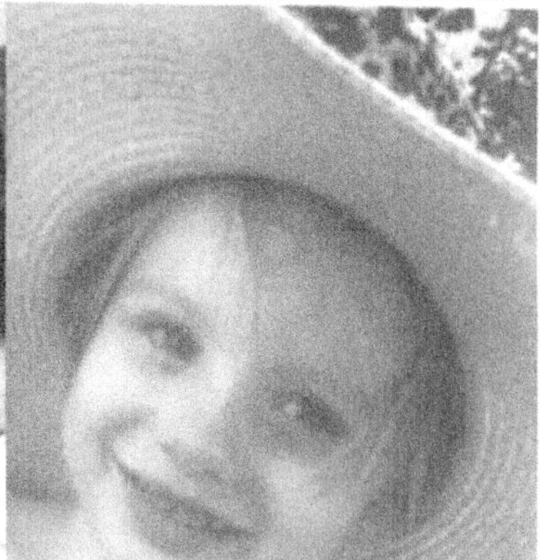

**September 2019.**
Skylar-Blue had just turned four and I remember thinking 'I don't want to leave them, I don't want to miss them growing up', 'I don't want to hurt my two best friends, why would I do this to Wednesday again and why would I put Ocean through this?'
Yet again I submitted myself into her arms, hating and writhing in this new heavier body, the problem was that people didn't notice so fast as I was still thin it gave me a head start in a way but the appointments continued and I hated that she was tearing down any progress I made but loved the buzz.

**October 2019.**
Me and October do not get on very well. It is either Asthma or mental health but either way we just do not get on. My weight continued to drop, and I was being more manipulative than ever before. The only problem was Dr Adcock and Dr Anwar still had tabs on me. I split the story and only revealed certain details to each Dr and Julie knowing that they would not be able to get the full story on how bad I was feeling. See, manipulation.
I sat there my heart beating out of my chest, I could not be bothered to do anything, yet Ana pulled me to exercise and to never stop. I had been permitted a small margin of rest that day but only if the scale read lower. I was able to lay my head down for 20 minutes before I was dragged back up on my feet. By this point I think I had given in all hope. I did not want to get better; I did not even care that I may not survive but I had to keep fighting.

I wanted to see my big sister get married. See this whole time I had been motivated by that one thought only highlighting Dr Anwar's faith that I would recover because even in my darkest I wanted to look well for my sister's wedding and what was even more, I wanted to look normal for 'when my nieces or nephews and my kids look back'... see that there 'my kids' I was looking forward. In some small sense I had not entirely given up and Dr Anwar highlighted that to me.

## A mother's point of view:

So Chlo was going down a slippery slope again and there was nothing I could do but watch and hope she stopped before it got too late.

You see, if I say anything I could a) Trigger her b) Knock her down when she was trying hard or c) she would think I had given up on her. It was a losing battle; I was damned for being damned.

So, I waited, secretly tried to count how many calories she was taking in, adding up and suggesting knew things to entice her to eat without letting on that I knew. A dangerous game and a balancing act.

Christmas as I have already said has always been our favourite time of year. So, when I noticed she was not getting as excited and was lethargic over the simplest things I was worried. Diet after diet adverts and always programmes on how to lose weight, eat healthier and get rid of 'excess fat' of which she felt she needed to! Of course, she did not as, as usual, she had consumed less over Christmas than all of us had. But she would not listen.

Photos are a sign for me because I can study them at leisure! It was late January and I started to see sunken eyes and a smile that did not reach them and slowly the cheekbones began protruding from her face. Her hair became lank with no volume or shine and I knew it would only get worse. My gut reaction was- No, no, no, I can't do this again, followed by, only seconds later 'Ok Ana, we've got this we've beaten you before we will do it again, you are not, repeat not taking my daughter away from me.

I will forever hate myself for that moment of weakness and self-pity. But isn't that part of the job? A mother's guilt is like no other!

March, she finally told us. Yes, if I am brutally honest, I was devastated, heart-broken and so incredibly sad. But I also knew how much courage and cajoling from Dr Adcock and Dr Anwar it had taken for her to tell us the truth. A few days later, Chloe told me, she thought it was best to recover on her own this time, prove to herself she could do it alone. You see, she was saving for a house with Josh, she wanted to move in with him. I was having none of it. No way could she survive a relapse without us behind her. I was so scared so very scared you see, I did not want her to go, I knew she had to. I knew what she was saying was true, but I did not want to believe it or accept it.

Over those awful years we had built and inseparable bond, so extraordinarily strong. Through her toughest years, then through my cancer. She was my baby, my last child at home. This emotion, I knew as normal. Do not get me wrong, I was devastated when Danielle left home too! We want them to spread their wings but then again, we want them to stay little girls forever.

So, this was her challenge at recovery. Her proof to herself and us, she could handle this disease on her own. Obviously, we will always have her back, but I knew she could do it. She has always been far stronger than she thinks she is. The arguments about food still happened but I did feel she was in control a bit more. Her doctors were amazing, and I felt she handled it better with them by her side. Plus, this took some of the pressure off of us as a family. I still went to work and poured my heart out to my friends who had been there all through the last awful recovery, they were and still are, amazing people, and give great advice. We also had a wedding to plan, and this was an amazing time for us as a family. So much to do, so Chloe got stuck in and helped her control-freak of a sister as much as she would let her! Wedding fayres, dress fittings and cake tasting! You name it and we did it. Chloe knew she needed to succeed for her sister. I didn't need to remind her, she was running out of time to get better, to look semi-decent on the photos . But most of all, not to have these photos stuck in time to show her she had been ill. She wanted, we all wanted to look back and have nothing but happy memories looking back at us through the photos. And she was doing it! It was painful, she always plays down her pain. But what I learnt through my own research and from Drs at Camhs is each organ has to re-grow in her body, every blood cell has to re-generate and the stomach has to slowly let more food in, too fast and it can cause more damage called 're-feeding syndrome', this is very dangerous, causing heart attacks and organ failure.

**A boyfriend's point of view:**

After hearing this chapter, I questioned Chloe on how I know if she is lying or not currently about her weight (06/11/2020) because as she has stated she is 'manipulative' when it comes to her Anorexia.

I was so angry when Chloe told me she had relapsed and even now I just do not understand it, I just feel like when it comes to recovery, she is full of crap. However, whilst I have no positives to tell here there were small moments of hope before it was 'oh no never mind she has done it again'. In France for example we made some good memories as she was normal again, we ate out and one place in particular comes to mind where we had burgers and things seemed like they were going to be ok. I feel very indifferent to this area of the story because I was swamped with Uni.

### A best friend's point of view:

When Chlo told me about her relapse I was crushed, my heart sank into my stomach and I thought 'I can't do this again' I honestly thought I would lose her last time and this time I thought it was inevitable and I didn't want to watch my best friend kill herself again. We didn't talk for a while partly because I was protecting myself but when I came back to Leicester (I moved to Hull) to see everyone I was shocked to see Chlo how I remembered her all those years ago. It was like looking at a ghost. I explained why I had not been around much, and she understood. Simply saying 'I don't think I can do it again so I can only imagine how you feel'.

I sat her down in Turtle Bay (a restaurant in Leicester city centre) and made her eat some chips, she does listen to me to an extent and then she stretched, and I saw every rib and pushed the rest of the chips towards her demanding she ate... she did. I knew she could fight it, but she did not she looked defeated. When I made her eat it was like permission and although she was teary eyed, she did it. She also ate a chicken nugget a few days later when me Ocean and the kids went out with her.

Once again we were on this journey and once again I believed in her yet I was terrified of losing her.

'Faith, Trust and Pixie Dust'.
-Peter Pan.

# Chapter Sixteen
# Disney works its magic.

So, Disney has this reputation of being 'the most magical place' and I can vouch for that a hundred percent. When I was younger, I went and Ana's voice was there but when we got to Disney, she did not make a peep and now at 22 years old we were off again.

It was the Hen party weekend for Danielle's wedding (one of them !) and we all travelled down in fancy dress apart from Auntie Anita, Mummy, Auntie Katie and Auntie Emma who opted for fairy wings instead (something to do with age apparently). I had done everyone a goody bag and was feeling like a good sister at this point, we did quizzes on the train about Danielle and then about Disney Princesses. I went as Belle, Danielle as Cinderella and Grace as Pocahontas which was no surprise as these are our favourite princesses. One of the other signs something was wrong was that the Tinkerbell costume I had bought for myself was too big on me and I had to give it to Amelie... I was now smaller than my baby cousin Obviously, there were others Elsa (sassy met sassy) but you don't need to have the list of costumes! I also made Disney T-shirts for the day at the park.

We sang going to the chapel on the way down on the train and eventually arrived at the park and settled into our rooms. I flung open my bag and the reminder was there as I stared at the fortisip's I had reluctantly agreed to. I stared at the snacks terrified that I would have to eat but I had been in recovery stage for a few weeks now and it was going well. Disney actually made it easy to ignore and I ate out pretty much finishing my plate a few times, lunch was hard, and I only managed fruit at this one place, but I did well.

I think the reason why I did so well was because a) it was wedding orientated b) Auntie Anita, Emma and Katie were there as support c) I didn't want Amelie to see what Ana truly did to me d) I wanted to see Danielle smile all weekend. Lisa was amazing with me as she always has been and talked sense into me when I needed it, in particular, on the first meal out that night. I realised how much I had lost when Amelie managed to pick me up the way I had picked her up as a little girl.

I had no access to anything other than walking, rides and fortisip's and in a way I had no room or time for Ana, I completely forgot for most of our trip. The only thing that interrupted the trip was my knee! I had done what me and Dr Anwar had agreed which was not to try so hard because that was why I would suffer mentally, through trying to get everyone to like me and to please them all. Through trying too hard I would get too sensitive and risk tensions etc, it worked but I had to battle with my Anxiety and the feeling that people hated me.

Danielle and I rode a few rides together and it was like being little girls again, her smile and laugh literally just brightened my day! Amelie and I rode the rest together and her hand holding mine reminded me more and more how much I wanted to be there to hold her hand through life as her cousin. Amelie being there was a blessing because I didn't want her to register any distress or behaviours, so I fought to hide it and stay normal although nowadays she knows and holds my hand or hugs me in those times. The biggest meal achievement was the first night because I had not done loads of walking, so it seemed unnecessary, but I had not as Auntie Emma and Lisa explained... I had not had much throughout the day to keep me going and I had still walked a lot. Danielle gave me one of her looks as if to say, 'come on you've got this' and I ordered my food eating nearly all of it IN FRONT OF PEOPLE.

Eating disorders bring a huge element of shame to food and eating especially when you do eat. They also make you feel like a failure and a sham as if those around you will think you're fat because you need to eat and often because you have to eat more (recovery). This was the case with the snacks I had to have around the park whilst others did not have too. On the final evening we went to watch the fireworks and I chose to have one of the toffee apples (it was a full on snow white vibe and beautifully made) we also had a glass of prosecco each that I treated D too. I wanted that weekend to be so special and memorable to her and it was, she had the biggest smile the whole time, she was home in a sense as were we both (we adore Disney).

**<u>A mother's point of view:</u>**

October came around, a year since NYC and we were off to Disneyland. What a magical time of year that was, what a wonderful place it is too. Now, I knew Chloe needed to eat and she also needed snacks and fortisip's throughout the day to keep her strength up. However, she did not want Danielle to know or for it to ruin the hen party by us reminding her to eat. Ingeniously we came up with a safe word, a word that we both knew meant 'eat', but without saying 'eat' or 'you need more food Chloe'. That word was... Tequila.

Disney was a success on all levels. Danielle had an amazing time, we have some wonderful memories and Chloe ate, she had snacks and her fortisip and even a Disney Toffee Apple (her favourite autumnal treat). She did not gain or lose whilst we were there, she maintained which is what her Drs wanted her to do. Laughter is the greatest cure they say, and I have to say, I believe it is. I honestly think that Disney came around at just the right time to help Chloe. Do not get me wrong, we weren't out of the woods yet, and we had another Christmas looming followed by a diet motivated January. But it was the boost she needed. The energy she stored up from all the love and support on those few days was enough to encourage her to continue to succeed.

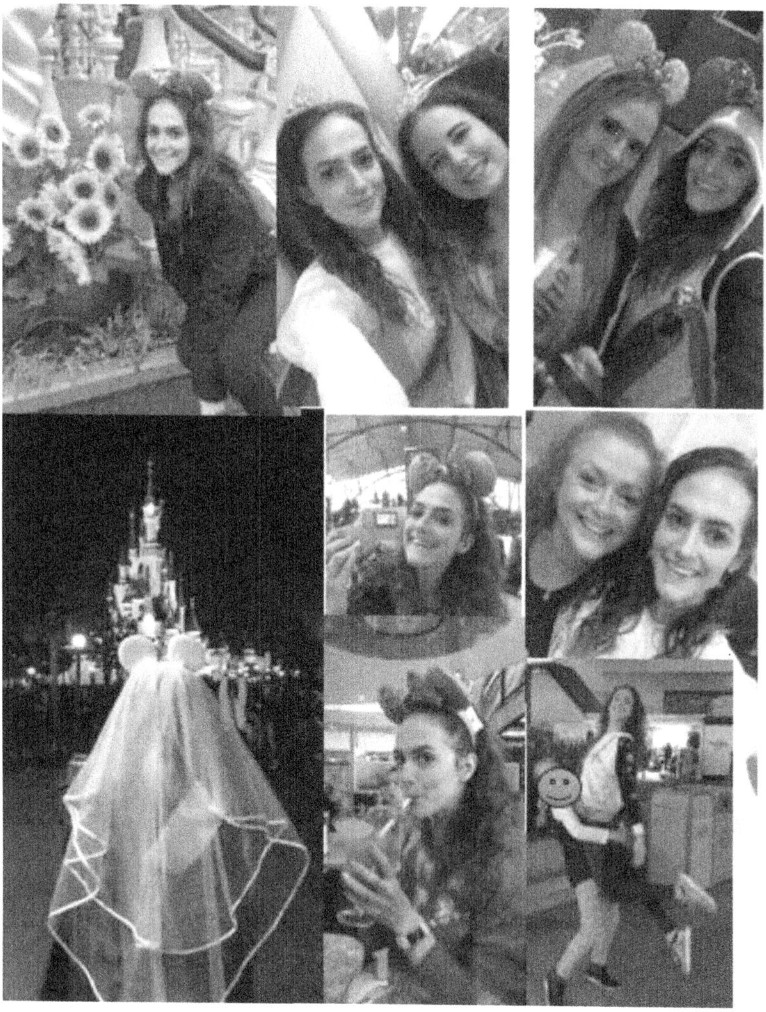

'If you aren't willing to keep looking for light in the darkest of places without stopping even when it seems impossible, you will never succeed'.

-Amelia Shepherd, Grey's anatomy.

## Chapter Seventeen
## Turn for the worst.

So, we had gotten back from Disney and things were going downhill again fast, I had stayed well for Disney but when I got home, I had lost a kg from all the walking around.

This is when I knew things weren't going well, the week after this I had gone for another appointment only this time I had water loaded in hopes that I would get away with what I was doing but I needed the toilet so bad that I ended up getting rid of half of it ! I shouldn't be here I thought to myself 'you're an embarrassment you shouldn't be here you vile waste of space, you fat failure you need to go, get up and leave' the voice bellowed in my head. I felt like I needed to lose more, that he would think I was fat which was ridiculous because there is no way he would have said that. If it were any other Dr (GP wise) I wouldn't be here, Dr Adcock knows me very well and he knows how to work around my bullshit and that is exactly why Ana is threatened by him. He called me in and I followed him through, the hallway was spinning like I was on a balancing beam, my heart was thumping and I was trying so hard not to faint because I knew if I did this weigh in would be so much worse than it was already going to be. My calories and tricks had been back to how they were if not worse and I knew he wouldn't be happy, 'what are we going to do with you?'.

I had the sick smile on where Ana shines through as the number goes down and I think Dr Adcock probably wants to join the queue of people who want to punch Ana if she was a real person but nevertheless, I pretended everything was ok. To be honest the night before I was so close to trying recovery because I had looked at my back whilst showering and that told me I was sick again. My bones protruded out; I knew they were because I was defensive about my parents coming in whilst I was in the shower which never usually bothers me. Despite the weight, despite the measurements my bones were telling a different story to what Ana wanted me to believe.

Anorexia is miserable so never believe for a second that anyone is in this situation by choice. I know there is this 'pro' community which promote this illness but that is beyond sick, there is a different sickness there that a) makes them believe it's ok to promote a severe psychiatric illness and b) is willing to share information and triggers to harm others.

When I was first in recovery someone messaged me on Instagram to warn me that there was one of these 'pro ana' sites using my image as what the sick twisted minds call 'thinspo' aiming for what nearly killed me, I was furious and after weeks of arguing them to take it down they finally did, I felt violated and guilty that someone out there had used my bodycheck as a goal. This, is why I am so against sharing bodychecks now, yes; they capture people's attention in media circumstances, but I have always asked to write something about it not being a goal etc. The only time I have ever used them are to create videos for myself to remind myself not to go backwards.

Food encompasses your every thought, instead of Uni I was drooling over 'sugar rush' and shows like that on the TV or watching people eat on YouTube yet again. Food, food, food! It is all you think about, how to avoid food, when to eat food and what to eat.

**<u>November 2019.</u>**

I walked to work with my heart fluttering in my chest, this would be my last day of work until I would have to get a Drs note declaring I could still work, my boss was amazing with it all, but I was caring for children it needed to be safe. My hands were cold, my emotions numb I knew if I cried it would not stop.

I saw mums with their babies, and I knew if I did not fix it soon then I would risk losing 4

that. I was a mess and I remember thinking 'things are bad Chlo, come on you have to do this, there's only so much the dream team can do without you'. I was at the point where I knew I had fucked up and that if I did not change soon no matter how much I begged Dr Anwar or Dr Adcock or Julie I risked going into hospital. I was chained to this demon, this stubborn child who had a tantrum whenever I so much as touched food.

Alanis was trying so hard to help but my resources were running out there was not much more anyone else would be able to do. I stood staring at myself in the mirror and the person staring back was not me anymore. It was her, glaring at me from behind my own eyes and it was haunting. Behind those eyes it was almost like I could see a little girl begging for freedom. A little girl who had been trapped for years and a young woman recently stolen from the world and put into that cage beside her younger self, begging for a saviour and begging me to fight for them and for myself. Following this Julie decided it would be beneficial for us all to have a joint meeting soon. 'Shit' I thought now the stories will come together and they will know everything.

I had retreated to my old world, the one that was cold and dark, the one in which I was merely alive and not living and now Ana feared for this joint meeting. My weight was dropping consistently along with potassium and sodium levels and something else beginning with a C or K that I am sure Dr Adcock would know! I debated skipping the meeting, but something inside told me that all three of them in one go would potentially free me from her claws just enough to grab the rope my family and friends were reaching out with.

The night before the meeting I went into my old room and sat looking out of the window. Looking for some advice from Auntie Rachel or Nanny but the sky was black, and it honestly made me feel like my time was running out. My thought process here was that maybe this tie to my past would remind me that recovery was possible. Part of me was excited for this meeting because it was a real chance for everyone to get together and sort things out. I had told Julie I was worried because I had split the story to protect myself and now, they would hear it all.

The day came around, December the 6th and big events were looming in the future that I needed to be well enough for. I walked in following Julie and Dr Anwar sat across with her 'it's ok' smile and Dr Adcock turned around noticing I was significantly thinner than when he had last saw me just two weeks ago and he made sure to say that. I sat in silence to begin with and I really just felt like I was looking down on the meeting. That was until Julie looked across at me urging me to get involved, I knew she knew pretty much all of it anyway so she could tell them regardless and so I joined in.

I told them I felt horrendously guilty because I had actually gotten to the point that when Skylar and Kien (fairygodbabies) were offering me food I was actually getting cross and saying no which wasn't me, Ana was taking that part of me now too and what was embarrassing was that I was too weak to even lift Skylar up. I had her for the day for one of our 'Auntie Coco and Skylar-Blue girlie time' and took her to the park whilst there I was mortified that I could not get her back out of the swing. My arms were too weak it took just about everything I had to get her out (luckily she found it absolutely hilarious), this along with what Dr Anwar, Dr Adcock and Julie were saying started to change my view on recovery and suddenly I had this strength and belief that I could do it, I had to do it.

Josh had had the idea the week building up to the meeting that because after meetings with either Dr Anwar or Dr Adcock I was ok for a while I should ask them to write 'eat' on a piece of paper for me to carry around with me as both a reminder and a push but also a type of permission to allow myself to eat. Both Drs basically said the same thing that we were at a point where if things didn't change I would have to be admitted, I didn't want this and then Julie had the idea that we all sign a contract that I would have AT LEAST two fortisip's a day on top of any food I happen to have. We wrote it out and all of us signed the agreement, surprisingly it worked, and I started to eat again slowly but surely there was improvement.

Luckily, the weight went on enough for me to have my knee operation, I had a patella femoral ligamentation transplantation surgery and it was without a doubt the most painful thing ever! But in the long run would mean I could work out and have some control over my body but two weeks later things just returned to how they were. Mainly because I am such a control freak and so I refused to look away when they had to do the pre-op weight and yep you guessed it, I freaked out!

**A mother's point of view:**

Christmas 2018, I saw some signs I recognised in Clo, just small little warning signs. Photos are a bit give away for me. I could see it in her eyes. I waited to hear the worse.

Jan 2019, diet adverts EVERYWHERE, all over the telly and magazines. There was no escape for Clo. She was surrounded.

When I realised, she was going back to Ana, my instant reaction was... NO, NO, No, not again, I cannot do this again, I am too tired

A second later, ok Ana, we have beaten you once, we will do it again, you are not, I repeat NOT taking my daughter away from me.

When she eventually told us in March, I knew we were on a long road to recovery. But something was different. I could tell she was not prepared to let Ana take over.... So, she would fight and fight for survival. All we could do was watch and support her.

The dream team were amazing and with us at home, we slowly managed to keep Clo going.

## A boyfriend's point of view:

Chloe was at least honest post Disney and told us how sick she was which is how I came up with the 'Eat' idea because she had told me how bad things were but that both Drs got through for a while.

Julie's idea of the contract was a really good idea, and it gave her a big boost because she was so intent on not letting them down that she stuck to it for the most part. The joint meeting was a really good idea and it helped her to make some real progress. She is a very stubborn woman and so when she does commit to recovery, she does it.

I was worried that her body wouldn't take well to the surgery and I knew money issues with Bipolar were another factor to worry about but the operation was done over Christmas and so she only missed out on a little work.

All in all things were looking up.

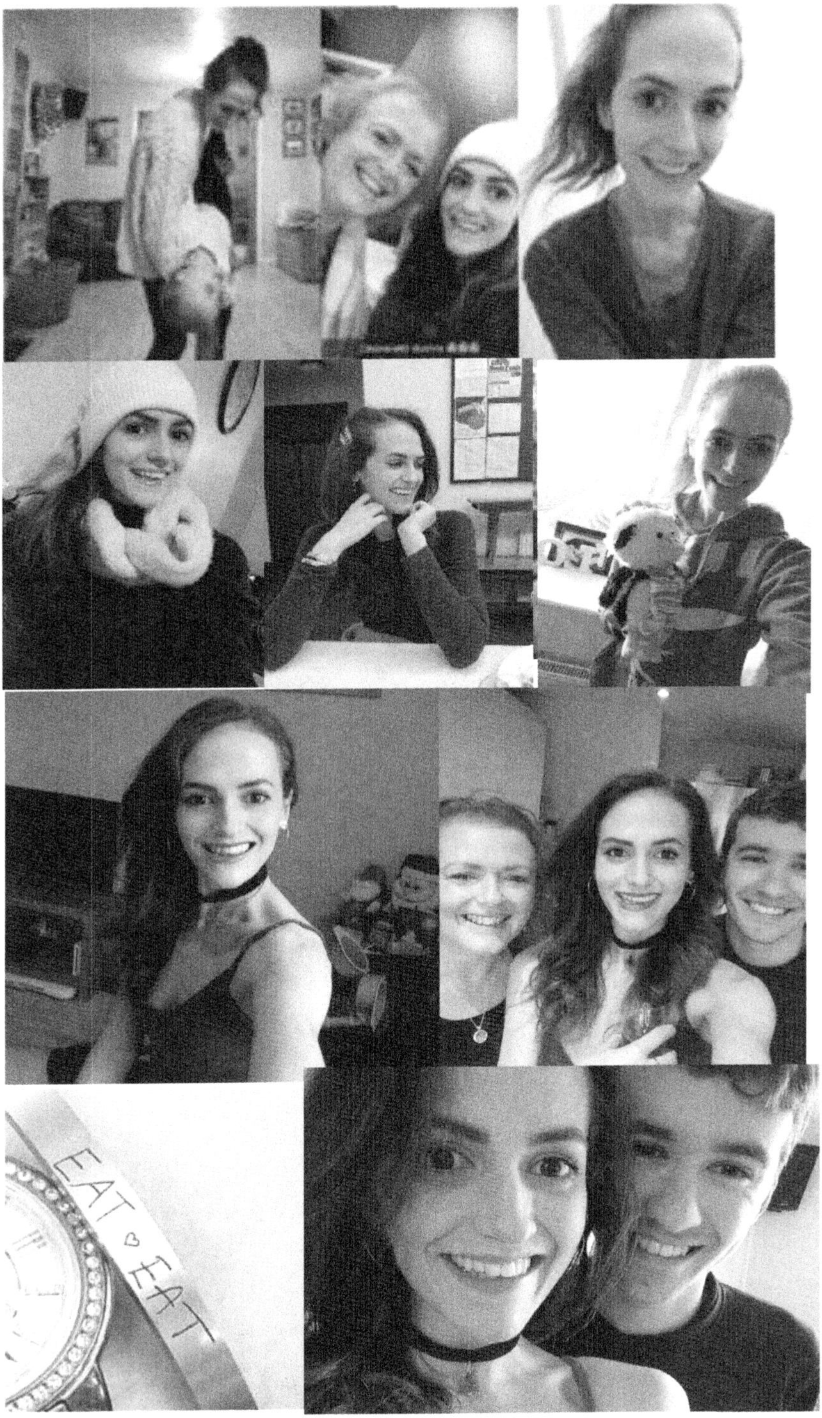
EAT ♥ EAT

'Resilience comes from adversity'
-Dr Anwar.

## Chapter Eighteen
## Amelie.

I named this chapter after my little glimmer of hope because it was a photo with her after my rainbows and brownies had their concert that hit me. That photo will always haunt me but bless me at the same time. I had agreed to the contract for help from the joint meeting a few weeks before and Ana was beginning to resurface so I was restricting again.

We had done the yearly carol concert with the Rainbows and Brownies (absolutely adorable) and we all went into the church hall afterwards to have mulled wine and biscuits etc. I had a glass of mulled wine and I was already feeling fuzzy but as I took the photo, I started to feel my legs give way. When my eyes refocussed, I looked at it and I saw what looked like someone who looked like me, but this girl wasn't quite her, her face was pulled taught and she was a ghost of that girl I once knew.

I looked like death, like a corpse. It was there that I thought and knew I needed to sort this for good. There was so much to look forward to, Danielle's wedding was only two months away and the weight had to go on to look normal in those wedding photos. I was also moving out of my parents' house and in with Josh which I knew I would mess up if I had to go inpatient or into a hospital. I knew I needed to work to get this house, I knew that I was passing uni but how I have no idea.

I will always feel terrible that Amelie had to grow up with me the way I was. She quite often got me eating a few bits here and there as like Skylar, Kien and Hallie I just cannot say no! There was one occasion where we went on a picnic to Foxton Locks ( in Leicestershire) and whilst there she must've been about 3 or 4 and she asked me 'Chloe' (or Coee as it was back then) 'why won't you eat anything ?' this broke my heart because it meant she had been picking up on my behaviours and I felt terrible about it.

When I got really sick back in 2017 I had to tell her I couldn't pick her up and she asked if she was 'too heavy now', I immediately got defensive as I have never wanted her to say anything like that even though it was an innocent comment. 'NO' I responded 'not at all, I just have a poorly heart' and what was even more heart wrenching was when I stopped taking food from her and I had to watch that little face get worried about me. When I got better in 2018 I did a photoshoot for my A-Level work and It was of me and her, I was picking her up and she said 'I'm glad you're better now Chlo, you can pick me up and swing me around again, I like that' . Honestly, kids can say the smallest things, but they are so observant and will tell you how it is with no filter at all.

As my relationship with Josh began to develop even more, she took to him so fast, she loved messing about and chatting away to him. We went out to a food fair once and he carried her on his back for half of it up until she wanted to try the clay machine on a stall because 'that is what Chloe does'.

By 2019, Amelie had known about what was actually wrong with me for about a year, I think she had figure it out herself as she learnt about growing up from books etc. I am not sure if she asked my Auntie and Uncle or whether they just knew she knew but either way she found out eventually. My family had started off being really unsure of my illness and didn't understand it at all, but the more time has gone on the braver they are at asking me about it and I think that's a really beneficial thing. Families need to be able to ask their loved ones how they feel in order to understand the mind of an Anorexic (or any other illness in fact). I remember when she came out with it, Danielle was in hospital for ongoing stomach issues and we were discussing medication and I had said to D that I'd had morphine with my appendix but Amelie had said 'did you have that because of your Anorexia?' I froze. It came out of nowhere and eventually we discussed the bipolar as well, the best way I explained it was simple and she understood it no issue ' sometimes I get really sad and I can't get out of bed or look after myself but then sometimes I get too happy and do silly things and so I take a special tablet to keep me in the middle' and now she knows pretty much everything.

I needed motivation to recover and I thought the best place to start was to make myself obliged to eat as well as what I had from Dr Anwar and Dr Adcock I decided to do challenges like some youtubers I had seen and because of my own channel I figured I would do the same.

Amelie picked pretzel fingers from a fresh pretzel stall in Highcross shopping centre and even chocolate sauce (pre anaphylaxis). Finley and Uncle Mark also challenged me as we spent some time together over the Christmas/new year period.

Christmas day I actually ate reasonably well for the first time in months and that little nugget (what I call her) was down to you. See Amelie has always been my rock without knowing it, whether it was cuddling her or eating what she gave me it just worked I could never hurt her, and I was hurting her by giving in. For Christmas Josh had gotten me a bracelet with both Dr Adcock and Dr Anwar's 'eat' writing on a bangle and I wear it a lot to remind me to eat and remind me it is ok to eat.

Even to this day my sweet girl will make me videos telling me how much she loves me, texting me when she knows I am in a bad place and always hugging me. She is such a special girl, and I cannot believe through all of this she has loved me. Over the years despite the age gap she is becoming a best friend much like Mum and Danielle became mine as I got older. The love I have for her has gotten me through some of my worst times. The times I have been suicidal and standing in the middle of roads, the times my bipolar has made me so low I've thought about nothing more than ending it yet this little girl needs me and so I fight.

I am now a cousin who will fight tooth and nail to be a part of her life and I will always protect her from what got me , I hate when she talks badly about herself and her body.

Because of that photo I started to fight again, and I was doing really well. I kept it up for so long. Well... until March, things were rough but the fortisip's were being drunk, the food was being eaten and the lies had stopped. The photo reminds me of my worst moment, the post appointment agreement providing me with hope and the photo shows that small glimmer it is also the first smile documented in months in which my eyes smiled too.

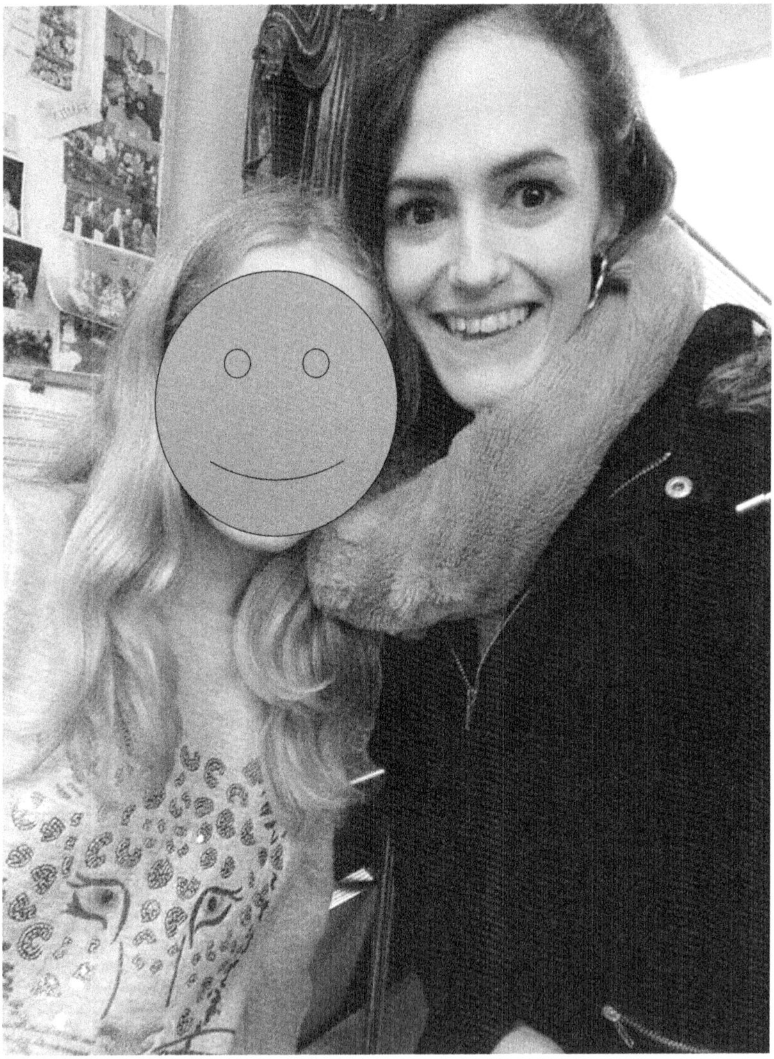

'Be the woman that little girl she thought she'd be, it isn't over yet'.

# Chapter Nineteen
# Wedding Bells.

The day was finally here February 15$^{th}$, 2020 and I looked well! I had done it and boy was it worth it, nothing has ever compared to seeing my big sister in her princess dress shining with happiness.

I'm getting ahead of myself, the year of prep had all been worth it, she tried on over FIFTY dresses until we finally found the one, she went full Cinderella which I knew she would and her wedding was magical. We had been to wedding fayre after wedding fayre and I had tried every food item needed because like hell was Anorexia getting anywhere near this special occasion.

The night before, we had a lovely meal at Mummy and Daddy's (I had moved out by then) and in the morning people had fruit, croissants and bubbles. I had fruit and a fortisip but it was nice to feel like I was normal, Danielle's friend and goddaughter also stayed and so I got lots of baby cuddles which really helped keep me calm. However, in all honesty Ana did not bother me all day, I was too busy doing my sisterly duties.

I was also mega excited to see Wednesday as her and her fiancé were coming to the evening party, she came to the church too and we had a quick hug before going in. Our makeup was gorgeous, and I had a lovely moment with Amelie where I painted her nails for her because the muppet had forgotten to paint her toes! Sitting around and chilling whilst makeup and hair was underway gave me the chance to really soak it all in and I have not seen Danielle that excited since Christmas as little girls but even that didn't compare to the excitement she had on that day. Her dream was coming true and she was about to put on her Cinderella dress, I was honoured when she asked me to come up and help Grace and Mummy do her dress up although I was terrified that I would do it wrong ! She walked down the aisle to 'circle of life' and our Brownies and Rainbows came to sing at the end.

It is moments like that when you realise what you could have left behind you, what you risk losing should you carry on in the way you are. I ate both courses at the dinner and even had wedding CAKE and CANDYFLOSS. I love candyfloss and yes I drank, in fact I thought I was fine until the taxi ride home where I realised I was definitely drunk, turns out you can be well mentally but your body still needs the recovery amount no matter what you're doing.

When we got home, I made myself a snack and ended up falling asleep on the sofa, bridesmaid dress and all! I had danced my feet off and not only that, but Ana was silent for the whole day even with wedding photos. My knee held up which was pretty good going and the time I spent with Wednesday was lovely, she was so proud of me and whilst I was significantly smaller than the last time she saw me she knew I was fighting because I was smiling with my eyes.

There were memories shared and a few tears for those who could not be with us. Danielle carried her bouquet with Auntie Rachels locket on and I made sure that the photo of her face them both the whole time which felt like she was here watching with us all. Danielle looked like an absolute princess although I still have no idea why she made us go out into storm Dennis for photos! There is a lovely photo of Danielle and Dean but what you cannot see is me behind them holding Danielle's veil down.

There are moments in recovery where you realise your body isn't back to normal yet and that's things like the cold and the wind where yes everyone is cold, but somehow you're colder to the touch than them or when everyone's dancing away but doesn't have to stop because they're a little dizzy even though they had a nice dinner earlier in the day. I had cake but a few people noticed the distress it caused me. However, yet again being surrounded by almost everyone I love, I was brave.

Bravery does not have to be you fighting alone, look around you because bravery can include allowing those around you to hold you up too. Bravery can be found not just in yourself but in those around you willing to fight beside you. They are brave and they are your source of strength and fight and if you allow them to, they can help carry you pretty much all the way.

What a day it was and what an honour it was to be her bridesmaid. I could not imagine and do not want to imagine what it would have been like if I was not there or if I was still visibly sick. I now know that should my nieces/nephews, sons/daughter's look at those photos they will not see Auntie Coco/Mummy as sick. They will see me for me, for my smile and my craziness and not for my illness. I cannot wait for the day I become an Auntie (to an extent I am with Skylar, Kien and Hallie (Ocean's babies)). I cannot wait for a mini Danielle or Dean running around with their HEALTHY Auntie Coco.

I am blessed to have a brother-in-law who has been like my big brother for almost 12 years and would do anything to keep my big sister smiling. Thankyou Dean, for making her happy.

'Thinking about doing something about your

situation is already a big step in itself; you know what to do'

-Dr Adcock.

'Embracing your natural beauty does not exclude anyone. There is no fine print. You can be naturally beautiful with acne, scars, cellulite or curves.'

-Lili Reinhart.

# Chapter Twenty
# New beginnings.

In February 2020 me and Josh got the keys to our first house together, we moved in as fast as we could as Danielle's wedding was the next weekend and all our family came over to look and help get it all sorted. Danielle came on day two and helped me finish unpacking and then we finished off with a domino's pizza ( I love pizza, especially dominoes) and this was the first time I'd had it since recovery had started. Leaving home was a big deal for me as I had been through so much with Mum and Dad and so I think I had some attachment issues with leaving. I also did not want to leave Twinkle (the cat), PixieBelle came with me obviously and we settled in fast. Now me, Dr Adcock, Dr Anwar and Julie all chatted about it in advance and I think there was a half and half worry between us all and that was that the independence would do me good or it'd make things worse. Guess which it was...

Yep! I got worse. You never want to lie but, in this situation, it was more weighing up whether a lie would protect my loved one and whether telling them would protect me or not. I did not want to hide it but neither did I want to admit it, truth was I did not think I could do it again.

I was tired and cold and frankly fed up with the same old routine, the same old patterns. I did not want to stay silent, but I also did not want to let them down and so .... I stayed silent (clearly, I was not understanding that by telling people I had a better chance). I tried to say it a fair few times, but my brain just would not let me, it is like a hand covers your mouth and mutes you.

Same chair, same room and same palpitations. Same prayer. That I will not have to go back to ED services and the I will not need to be admitted. What would he say? Would the food I ate be enough to weigh me down? I thought, I had allowed myself an apple in hopes that it and the water would weigh me down (see how irrational the thought process is?). I wanted the day to be over so badly at that point, everything hurt, everything inside me felt like it was being torn to shreds by the wildfire that is Anorexia, screeching through my brain and ripping my soul to shreds. She had gradually pulled me back into her grasp and the problem is that each time she does it her grasp gets that little bit tighter and the battle becomes harder. My weight had dropped yet again and all I wanted to do was curl up into a ball and sleep the days away.

Sleep is the only peace I get and sometimes Ana finds me there too. The fear of a new day is harder to accept than any level of pain I was in because I knew in 12 hours it'd all start again, the same hollow pit, the same loneliness and the same insatiable need to starve.

It is only me that lives in this hell hole not them, it is me in the hell I have the pleasure to call my life. I think Dr Anwar knew early on that things were going downhill again, and she had told me that my potassium levels were worrying her again. I remember her telling me that any lower and I would have to go in and that she did not want to come and see me in hospital. Another day meant another onslaught of abuse and I was hiding my food, measuring food and I was just all in all a complete mess, walking as much as I could and doing everything in my power to lose more and more weight and what was even better... Josh didn't know. Ana loved how inexperienced he was with living with an Anorexic and she thrived with it. We thought I was sick in December oh how we were wrong.

What has kept me going is the dream of having kids and I knew after taking a waist measurement that something had to give, I needed the periods back if I stood any chance at all. I needed to be taking my fortisip's and yes, I love the bone and I love the low numbers, but I knew that in order to recover I would have to leave those behind. I wanted to change but I did not want to change, I was at a crossroads. It's that sick need for visible protruding bones, for lower numbers and thinner legs, arms, tummy you name it and there is Ana every single time, coaxing me back to the insanity that is in fact my sanity.

There is nothing stranger than feeling your body crumbling through lack of fuel that you're putting inside of it but then each time. I tried, it was like my body was rejecting it, my stomach hurt to hell, my chest felt tighter, my heart got louder and I felt violently sick and often was sick despite the little I was eating.

The alarm went off at 7am for me to go for my morning walk and so I dragged my bony body up and took my bodychecks, Josh was at work and so I did 10 sets of stairs, I fought through the pain, through the heart ache knowing that everything she ever promised me and everything she would keep promising me was and always would be a lie. What would be achieved every time... misery. There is no point in the depths of my anorexia that have I smiled about running up and down stairs, I have never smiled about the wobbly legs or anything she gets me to do in fact even when the number drops its milliseconds before the misery returns.

Dr Adcock and Dr Anwar were both on at me about my weight and potassium (thank you guys!) and Julie was my vent for how overwhelmed I was and then all of a sudden things got very real as they were both very blunt about where we were headed. I thought it was just a scare factor to be honest but then in March it happened... lockdown (the only good bit of COVID).

Now, I was having some ambivalence anyway as I did not want to keep lying to Josh, I felt horrendous about it and now much to Anas dismay, he was to work from home. FUCK I thought, how the hell do I get away with this now? I tried so hard; this was when I knew things were not going well at all. Whenever I tried to eat, I felt unbelievably sick, was it my brain refusing to let me eat or my body? How was I supposed to do this if each time I tried it would be like this? I had to remind myself I had done it before. With lockdown the Drs shut and Dr Adcock had told me how serious my state was as they were 'only doing emergency blood tests' suddenly I realised I was sick and with a pandemic there was no way he would be using scare tactics now and the same with Julie and then Dr Anwar.

It was time to try this recovery thing again, so the bracelet( with EAT on ) went on and I stuck the contract on the fridge, put on my armour and went to battle the bitch yet again. Dr Anwar had told me not to do any YouTube challenges this time that maybe Ana was letting me challenge myself so that I would then be overwhelmed and go running back to her (now for someone who keeps telling me I know more than her about Anorexia, she seems to know more than me and Ana does not like it).

I lay in bed repeating the same quotes 'resilience comes from adversity' and 'ambivalence is not necessarily a bad thing' , It was 3am and this was my exercise time, I was trying so hard to not get up into the spare room to work out, it was as I call is Ana's witching hour. I knew I should be sleeping but I also knew I should be burning calories ... this was going to take some getting used to! I did not want to turn on my body just yet, I wanted to give it just a little more time, to see how it will cope and whether it will be on my side of not

April came around and it was my birthday, I was miserable knowing I could not see anyone, but I was making real progress. Fortisip's twice a day with food as promised had my Anorexia quaking in fear. Josh wrapped up my presents and we ordered in for dinner (a huge challenge and the meal was disappointing; the restaurant is shut down now... guess that tells you about the food). Mum, Dad and Danielle came over and sat opposite ends of the driveway, so we all had about 3metres between us if not more. They had their own prosecco glasses and the only thing we all touched was the bottle! Mum had made me a cake WHICH I had some of (my favourite... lemon) and they gave me my presents. I finally got a weighted blanket from my Auntie Katie and it was a god send.

A few weeks went by and it was going so well and then there it was as I sat wracked with guilt over what I had eaten despite it still being low for a 23 year old woman I feel a dull ache, I didn't want to jinx it so I stayed quiet but something felt familiar. It was heavy and dull, and this familiar feeling was not going away, I was praying to God it was what I thought it was. My body breathes a sigh of relief as it finally trusts me again, my period was back.

**A mother's point of view:**
So, the weekend finally arrived, and Chloe was moving out. She was leaving. My brain was in turmoil, I wanted her to be independent, but I had a niggling feeling Ana would show her ugly head.

I pushed these feelings away and decided to stay positive, well for now at least. I had a wedding the weekend after!!!

Wow what a day that was, all of my family together celebrating my beautiful daughter getting married. Such lovely memories that will stay with me forever. Plus, Clo looked amazing and I watched her enjoy her day.

Unfortunately, lockdown arrived a month later, I was ow really concerned with Clo as I was not overseeing her food intake. She looked frail.

She looked ill

Her eyes were sunken.

I realised, to my horror that my worries had come true. The evil bitch was back.

Now, the temptation to scream at your daughter and ask why? Is overwhelming, but futile. It is not Clo, it ever is.

But something was different this time, there was a resilience in Clo I spotted that I had not seen before. She knew she had to fight it.

You see, wanting children and getting married always seemed such a long way away, so going back to Ana was OK, because she still had time tight?
No, not now, suddenly the time was coming bearer. There really was not long. She had already moved in and starting "adulting"! Time was creeping up on her. I could see it.
Yes, she had relapsed, but this time of going nowhere, had made her and Josh so much closer. They bonded without the influence of outside world.
She started turning it around. Her doctors were amazing and between them, Josh and us, she pulled through. Slowly. She did it. She had conquered Ana on her own. Showing her resilience and determination to live.
I am so immensely proud of her and all she has had to deal with in her life. I know I am biased, obviously, being her mum. But she is a strong, stubborn and beautiful young lady, who has such a fun packed exciting life ahead of her. The journeys from now on will be good ones, a few hiccups are ok. We are all human. But she has got this. I truly feel we have seen the back of this deadly disease. I live in hope we have.

**A boyfriend's point of view:**
Hearing that Chloe was exercising in the spare room honestly makes me feel violated. It shocks me how deceitful she can be when in the throes of her Anorexia, but I was proud of the steps she was making towards recovery.

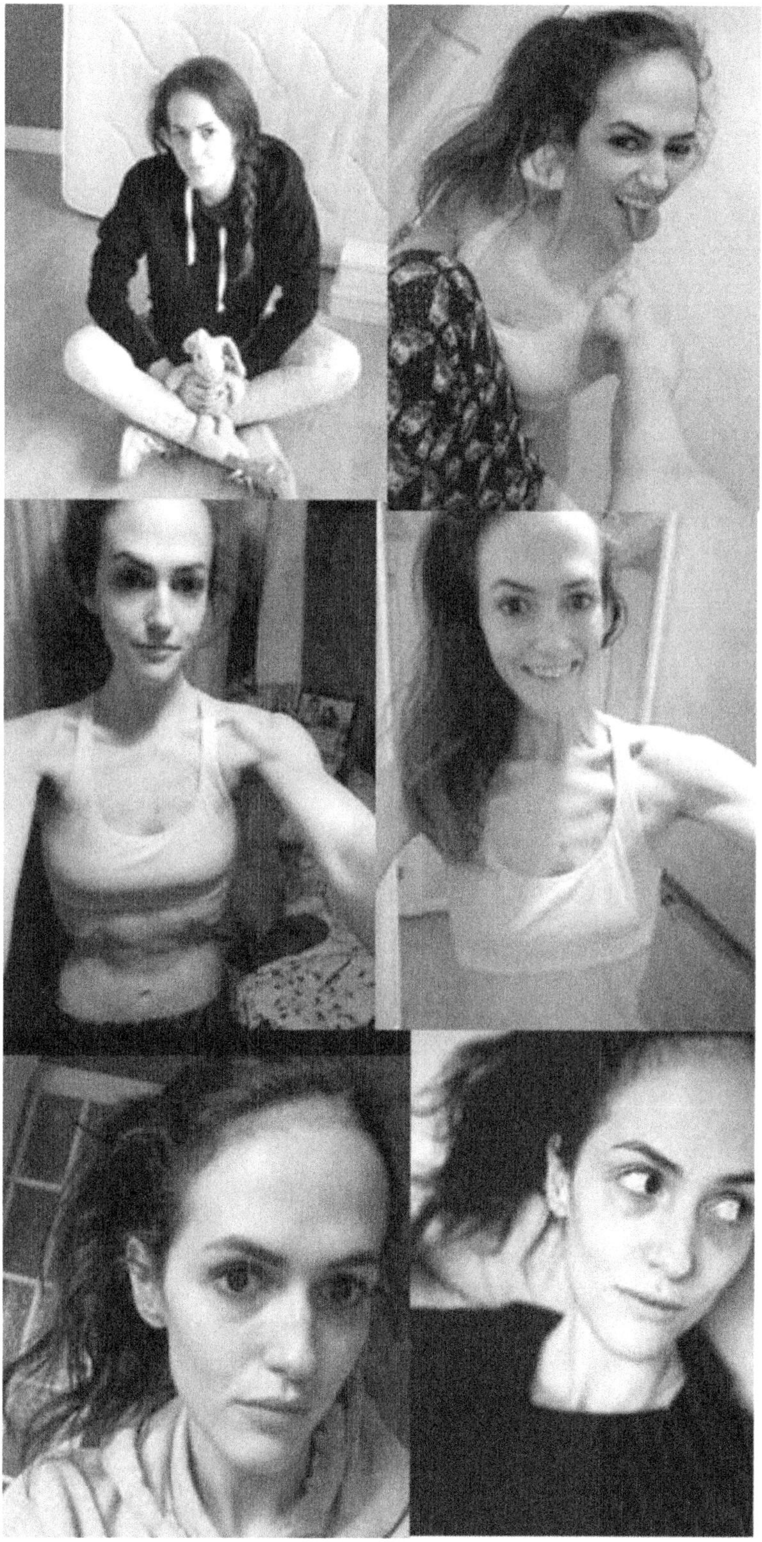

'Nothing is impossible, the word itself says
I'm possible.'
– Audrey Hepburn

# Chapter Twenty-One
# I'll Come Back Stronger.

That day is another date that will stick in my mind March 13th. The day I decided to change, to move away from it all again. To fight but all I could wonder was 'is it too late?' But through the cold nights, the pain and heartache that anorexia brings, I found myself wondering... what was it all for? What was I gaining through this writhing pain, what was remaining? If not the peace that Anorexia had promised, then what else was left? It was all a lie and I had known that for many years but never been brave enough to walk away.

One of the things I had to let go of was my Fitbit as this fuelled my anorexia, they weren't much of a thing when I was first sick but now my life revolved around 10,000 steps and a certain number of burnt calories, flights of stairs and this was not healthy. Luckily I had lost mine post knee-op and so Mum had said she would give me hers which we agreed on but that we would wait until I got better, well, enough to handle it without guilt. Unfortunately, what many people do not understand is it is calming, and many sufferers rely on it as a coping mechanism to soothe their stress or difficult emotions. Unfortunately, this would be my downfall, in October (see yet again with bloody October) after a string of Anaphylactic reactions in and out of ICU etc I just could not handle food. The more I panicked, the more food I stopped eating and then before I knew it, I was critiquing my body. See 'Hip-dips' were all over the internet and I could not help it when I saw any element of that, I saw fat.

It is like a weight on my shoulders, right in the middle of my once sharp protruding shoulder blades. Although they still showed, the sharpness had started to disappear, and it felt alien. My once frail body was beginning to fill out and become stronger, as much as I have pride in my recovery and the resilience of my body I could not help but crave my skeletal form, it feels pure and now I felt like a fake. How sick minded is that? Feeling fake because my weight is no longer (NUMBER ALERT) under 100, the pain I felt in my body was merely psychological, the thought of food entering my body, coursing through my body and providing it with energy disgusted me. I dreamed of the body I am striving for, my recovery body. Toned and beautiful yet beauty seems so bizarre when all I crave/d is my frail sick frame. I crave/d the high that starvation gives me, the ethereal sensation of being weightless.

My clothes were beginning to fill out and I hated it, I love the baggy and frail appearance and now I was curvy, and I could not stand it. My brain was seething with anger and hatred.

You can tell yourself all the lies in the world "I'll be ok" or "it'll be fine" being my particular favourites but sitting in Majors in the hospital I was born in because I took too many diet pills takes the biscuit. I mean when I get obsessed with weight I truly do; I will weigh everything I am wearing before going to the Drs for weigh in. Including water consumption so that I know when I've water loaded and slapped the layers on what the true weight is.

Dr A knows this so will weigh me just leggings and sun top, he clicked on my trick's years ago.

October 28th and I had no idea how to tell my parents or Josh for that matter that I was restricting again, I was sent home from work as I nearly passed out. Mum picked me up and I had to eat but when I got home, I was only being mentally and physically punished. I had also found a certain supplement that can encourage weight loss of which I had just finished and hoped I would not buy any more. Dr Adcock, Dr Anwar and Julie had been so supportive but the guilt I had about relapse was so strong.

We had a joint meeting three weeks before with Josh, he came in after we had talked about the Anorexia. Dr Anwar asked him how he thought I was doing (mainly regarding Bipolar as I'd had a manic episode recently), I sat with Josh in our first joint meeting and he said life was "normal" and I felt so guilty sitting there knowing I was not eating enough (sorry). I teared up a little, Dr Anwar gave me a small smile basically telling me it was ok and we went home.

I was in the car for work and I could not get my mind off how to avoid the next meal, but I knew it would only end one of three ways if I got worse. 1) I would be admitted 2) I would die 3) I would recover again; she has such a hold on me and who knows why.

I did not want to give in, and I did not want to be one with her, yet she refused let me go. Why she chose me I do not know, it makes me so angry that I fall for it every time. See I know her agreed weight will lower when I reach it, the allowed food going in gets less yet she pulls me along with her.

An apple a day they say. Well I had managed some breakfast because it would have been too obvious if I skipped and I had an apple in my bag with no intention of eating it. The scale whispered my name and I found myself seeking one out like a drug addict seeking their next high. I wanted to watch the number plummet, what caused it was the hip dips, society had/s been focussing on and so I became fixated on them too.

My family is curvy, so it is natural I will head to that, but I did not seem to be able to accept that. If there was a way to be healthy but still skeletal (sigh) I wanted that, but do I really want to be skeletal? No. I wanted my early recovery body back where my legs were still thin, and my waist still tiny, but I now had a glow of health not a dullness of death. I bought raspberry ketones to help the loss and I regretted it instantly, yet I could not change my mind now because I have bought them, how could I have been so selfish and stupid.

My new job started that Friday, just a simple shop job as I finish University, but I saw it as a way to exercise, to lose more by being busy and skipping those few snacks or meals. See my snacks had been eliminated weeks ago unless evening snack is around Josh but again, I had managed to go undetected when around him and been able to skip.

I had palpitations that had started already and the dizziness, my body was getting less able to handle it and it was kicking off. Yet how could I stop when everything inside told me to carry on, lose a bit more, just a few more kgs, a few more inches, just a few less calories.

It would be ok, 'it will not happen to us, we will be fine' she says. Remember the potassium issues I told myself, remember the sodium and the one I cannot remember I told myself, yet she managed to make me completely complicit to her ways.

Let us talk about working out for a minute, shall we? I am terrible at working out UNLESS I am in my Ana ways. Seriously, I am hypermobile so whenever I do it, stuff just hurts or dislocates yet when I am sick, I can whack out 100 crunches despite the back pain or 50 push ups despite the shoulders dislocating! Do not even get me started on how the hell I managed squats because I can go for hours, knees dislocating and all. Yet when I am in remission or recovery my knees just cave! They are the worst as we have established.

*October seems to be the time for my relapses...*

## 24/10/2020
I weighed myself a week after my appointment with Dr Adcock and it was a hefty loss. I realised I was yet again in over my head but the truth is I couldn't/can't stop myself and I'm too tired to fight again I keep thinking but as I write this I know I will find my strength again. I told Wednesday, Ocean and Clare (my best friends) and so I have their support at this point. all I can do now is pray to God that I fight this before it gets worse.

## 28/10/20
Dr Adcock called to check how I was doing and he told me that he will keep an eye but after seeing me through this for many years sometimes I 'bounce back' and that I am 'resilient'. I felt like a fraud because as Dr Anwar would say 'recovery isn't linear' yet I speak out about surviving this disease still facing its's abuse over and over . A friend from work encourages me to keep writing as a way of showing how you can have hiccups but still bounce back.

'You look pale' Mummy said the night before, 'shit' I thought to myself, does she know? She must know, she is seen it too many times I thought to myself. Then I got the lecture 'you are not eating enough to be working as much as you are', Ana gets defensive... back off Mummy I feel like screaming, you are rattling the beast. I am the hostage here do not make her fire the gun I thought.

Numbers, it all comes down to numbers, just get to ** and you can stop and get better, you made it now ** and then you can get better. What is the point? I sat in A&E after overdosing on raspberry ketones, this is something I have never done. I felt horrendous because there was nothing more that I would have rather done than to run into Josh or Mummy's arms and tell them I am not ok but Ana pulls me back each time I go to speak because they'll 'ruin everything' and so I could not.

I argued with a nurse because I explained that the scales you come in on with the ambulance were wrong and my paramedic said I could weigh on the other scales. She quite rudely said 'there's already a weight for this woman' I tried to explain but she walked off, luckily, they found me some and low and behold there was a 2kg difference in weight. Anorexia and I breathed a sigh of relief.

In the build up to that evening I had taken the ketones when I had gotten home and my friend Alanis came over after, we had a lovely catch up and before that Josh's brother Matt , me and Josh had a dominos which is my favourite treat but it was hell . The wine did not help my overdose and before I knew it, I had palpitations and severe stomach pain. I had, had a lovely time with everyone so why? I do not know. I was just in autopilot, when I came around and thought 'oh fuck' it was too late same as the 'oh fuck' when buying them.

I had become really poorly and oramorph was the only relief, luckily the Dr gave me the all clear and off I went. The guilt and fear I have in telling people was too much to bare. I could hear the arguments now, the disappointment and the guilt. Thing is, it is the disease, it takes over but also, I knew I could not keep doing this. At some point I **HAVE TO WALK AWAY** for good I told myself because I can honestly say she'll keep pulling me down until I become a ghost of myself and eventually die because let's face it, if she has her way that's where I will be. I was not as visibly unwell as I had been because I was on the way down but when I was in tighter clothes or naked, I looked 'like you've lost weight'.

Dr Adcock told me he is not 'too worried' at the moment as I have been here before in limbo and bounced back eventually but he says I am a 'resilient young lady' and he has faith in me. I want to love the world, I want to be good, to be something people can be proud of and at the minute I am just not is all I could think. I want to be a Mum, but it is different saying that now than years ago because now I am 23, having a baby and weddings are not so far away anymore. I am not loving myself, not loving the world the way I was born to and in the words of Meredith Grey 'life shouldn't be this hard'.

' I'll get to \*\* then stop and get better' I want to shake myself and shout 'It won't stop until you stop' what is the point in playing the game , what is the bloody point if I will always have to undo the pain anyway ?! I look at celebrities that I look up to so much who are normal and not what my brain wants me to be (Demi Lovato, Lili Reinhart, Holly Willoughby, Ellen Pompeo, Madelaine Petsch, Anna Saccone and Caterina Scorsone just to mention a few). I am really starting to hate the word 'relapse'.

## 04/11/20

Relapse is bitter sweet, you get this relief and joy that you have this power and control, that you can lose weight quick but you also don't want to let go of what little hope is left. Where's the book made for Chloe Shelton that says "your bones must be on show before you can love yourself, If your bones are covered you're to feel utterly disgusting and uncomfortable" and "you must totally rely on Anorexia and lie to those around you to fix it yourself but actually not fix it yourself because you're not strong enough"? I have no idea what to do, where is the book that tells me what to do and how to survive this??!

Oh, and have I mentioned that on this specific day today I had stood on three different demons sorry my mistake "scales" and EVERY SINGLE ONE read different. How fucked up is it that we pin everything on a number that changes depending on which plank of plastic or glass we stand on and what it tells us?! See she will not stop until she takes that last breath from me. She won't stop until she gets everything, all of me, she wants my skeleton yes but nothing else, not me, not the personality nothing just the bones inside, I sat debating whether to try and eat something or not. I knew I should because I had an endless stream of uni work to do and I needed the fuel. Here we go I prepped myself, deep breath and snack time it is.

Dr Adcock rang and said his famous phrase 'what are we going to do with you?' he had contacted Dr Anwar about my overdose as well. I told my boss about my relapse and yet again she was lovely. I was cooking the boys (I Nanny remember) their dinner and it was Pizza, my favourite and my nose was invaded by a wave of pizza scent. It was torture, my body craved it, it craves any nutrition, but my brain refused it would not let me even consider a bite.

## 05/11/2020
It is so hard to even manage a morsel and I hate myself the second I do. I sat regretting my idea to have smores as a date night bonfire lockdown celebration, there was salmon for dinner and I love salmon but my brain said no because it is a 'fatty' fish, even though it is a healthy fat. I had a phone interview for closer and I chatted to Kya the journalist who helped me so much as I told my story I realised how far I had come and so I had a snack which was a huge step. This was the second international lockdown as a result of COVID and unlike the first one it did not do me any good in fact, it made things worse, I realised this is was a never-ending cycle if I keep going back. At the end of the day I knew damn well I was going to get worse, then I would either end up in hospital or getting better. Either way the weight would have to go back on because I cannot live like this forever.

## 06/11/2020
I was stuck in this fight yet again, I was repeating Dr Anwar's phrase 'ambivalence is not necessarily a bad thing', I was weighing both options instead of completely writing it off. Why would I want to undo all the hard work I have done? But do I really want this life?

I ate the salmon the night before and it was beautiful, we had our own little bonfire and roasted marshmallows for smores. The guilt hit in immediately after the smores, but I went to bed telling myself I would restrict again tomorrow. My body check reassured me my body was losing weight, the bones were back, and I was high on the knowledge that they are protruding, I feel safe.

I ate pizza! my favourite food and although I could have eaten more (Anorexia approves only two slices) I felt normal. I even ate homemade gingerbread; I knew a lot of my eating was due to an upcoming period which I would end up missing this period due to weight loss.

**09/11/2020**
I cannot begin to explain how confused this disease can make you, do I want to recover? am I just feeding my body because of University assignments or am I trying?

As the day's food consumption loomed over me, I open a bottle of cider to silence my mind. I knew I had eaten because of a period but to me that is no excuse and never happens, so I turn to drinking. This is an unhealthy coping mechanism that unfortunately I seem to have developed over the years with my bipolar and it manifests itself now in my Anorexia too. Bipolar and Ana are best friends you see so they feed and fuel eachother in order to make my life a living hell.

**12/11/2020**
I told Josh I was struggling. I couldn't bring myself to say I had been restricting, the only thing I could do now to distract myself from Ana was to clean, write the book or watch Greys anatomy (again), why ? because in cleaning I feel like I can clean the negativity out of my life (Mrs Hinch is right!) , by watching Grey's I get to see healthy actresses and inspirational quotes (and it is amazing) and the book...well the book reminds me that there is a story to tell and I have to be here to tell it so it keeps me holding on.

**17/11/2020**

Post hospital after another anaphylactic reaction this time to fat metabolising pills. I was so embarrassed when I had to tell the ambulance crew this is what I had taken and again I had to hide it from Josh which made me feel horrific but when he binned them I wasn't angry at myself but at him. How dare he take away what could help me lose this weight? I had missed my period which tells me my weight loss was too fast and my body has had enough again as I am as regular as clockwork. Whilst in hospital I hardly ate but the nurses were so good when they found out how bad my anorexia was and had been that they pushed me towards eating. I left feeling like I wanted and needed to change and when I got home I decided it was time to embark on changing my life for the better... again. I decided to order a crystal water bottle for positive energy which thanks to Clare (Kit car member) I have benefitted from in the past and decided to take care of my body because it is true in the very cheesy way that we only get one body and I am fed up of abusing mine. I came home and ate a decent dinner and night snack.

**18/11/2020**

I was so worried I would run away from recovery the next day, but I had a decent breakfast and what is more I had a fortisip too! My first fortisip in months and my body instantly showed signs of relaxing. I worked away on my university which I find difficult when I am not in restriction but I was determined to make this work, determined to exercise healthily and eat a balanced diet because I cannot have children or live happily with Ana controlling everything. Having said that, the guilt and nausea I face/d is horrendous but that is to be expected as my brain wants me so badly to starve.

## 20/11/2020
Things since hospital had been heading in the right direction. There is this niggle inside of me however that tells me to stop. Stop eating, stop trying and lose the weight but after a chat with Eddy and Ocean as well as seeing my gorgeous fairygodbabies over video call I realise this is what I want. Not a life of starving until admission risk and then getting better before doing it all again and so it is time for me to walk away from my habits. Yes, I will probably always suffer with my anorexia, but I refuse to let it take over my life, I refuse to keep doing it.

## 23/11/2020
I had been eating on a schedule for almost 4 days and I was ok with it. The day before was tough and I wanted so badly to skip meals, but Josh ate with me for dinner and made me feel ok with any extras. My dietician had been in touch as had Julie and they both got me on track. Gloria (my dietician) explained that I keep giving my body nutrition for a bit but then I abuse it again and leave it back at square one! This made me feel even worse for my body, I have been abusing and torturing it for years and just when it thinks it is over I do it all over again!

## 01/12/2020
I am getting there slowly, I think. It was ok at 17 when I said I wanted to get better to have children because I had a long time to get better until then, but now the idea of having children is becoming more and more of a reality it is getting closer ! So, I think it's nearly time to end this book and the ambivalence throughout this chapter is perhaps the best place to leave this because ambivalence is the most realistic place in recovery for me and for many others. I believe I am ok and I have to believe that life can be more than just numbers and bones.

Thing is Ana, the life I deserve is mine, my own making and my own future.

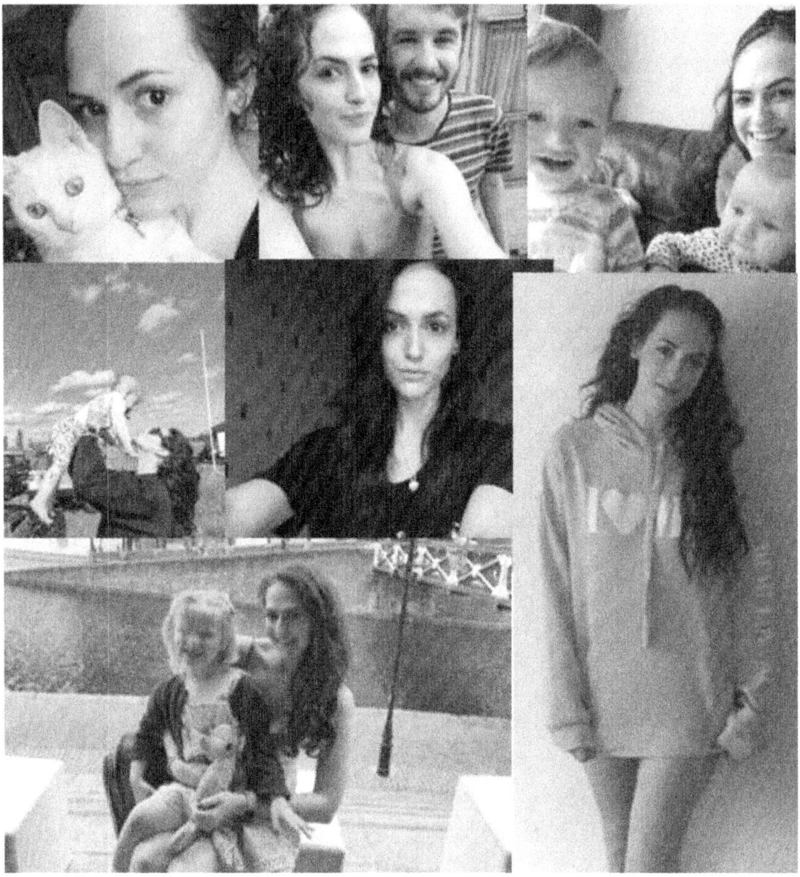

'It's not hard. It is painful but it's not hard. You know what to do already. If you didn't you wouldn't be in this much pain'.
- Miranda Bailey,
Grey's Anatomy

# Chapter Twenty-Two
## Advice.

Life can throw so many hurdles at you, sometimes you may feel it is happening to you more than anyone else, I know I sure have. However, it is ok to feel that way because it doesn't matter what happens to you it is the way we deal with it that determines how our life will go.

Anorexia is not easy, trust me I know, and I know it can be the best most calming solution you can think of but trust me when I say that it'll come to an end. The stress will catch up with you eventually, so it is down to us as individuals to find a healthy coping mechanism. I have found this hard especially with my Bipolar and self-destructive tendencies but eventually you will find one that works for you, yes some of them will fail but you will find a way it's just about pushing through and remembering even if you're in no mans land and cannot decide whether to recover or not 'ambivalence is not necessarily a bad thing' you are making steps just by thinking about it.

I think one of the best things I could've been told in my darkest time of relapse when my whole life felt like it was falling apart and my thoughts were all over the place was that I wasn't failing at all because, through the pain there was this nagging debate on whether to take that first step or not.

You just have to have courage to take that journey, what is worth remembering is what I can guarantee you've probably heard but hopefully coming from a fellow sufferer may help. YOU ARE NOT IN CONTROL, you may think it, maybe even feel it, but this will end one of two ways unless you pluck up the courage and fight 1) you will die, it will end the way your disorder wants it to or 2) you will have the control completely taken away by those trying to save you. No matter how many times you come in and out of hospital with it the cycle will continue because people around you will not want to lose you.

The pain that comes with recovery is unbearable I will not lie. I wish someone would have told me. You will want to crawl back to restriction instantly because it feels easier, but the pain means it is working, I remember telling Dr Adcock about the pain and do you know what he said? 'that's a good thing'. I was so confused! Why is pain good? Then he said 'it means it is working, it's a good pain, nothing bad is happening your body is healing' then I thought of the scene in Harry Potter where he has to go through all that pain when he re-grows his bone and it made sense. I ended up having to give myself a pep talk, 'it's ok Chlo, it's going to be ok, you won't die, you won't be fat overnight and your body will make it through. The pain will not last forever and there is so much left we can do in life'.

Another thing I wish someone would have warned me about was the friends that will turn on you for speaking your story, they are not worth your time, let them go , you are not made to please everyone. Speak out about your journey if you want to, speak out in pride because you are a survivor but if you do not want to then that is fine too you do not owe anyone anything. Be you, be fearless and be yourself because there is no one else like you, no one who smiles the way you do or laughs the same as you. You are a limited edition, one of a kind... you are perfect.

There is no sense in pleasing everyone because it just is not possible. I suffered and still do suffer mentally with trying to be liked by everyone but as my work colleague says, 'fuck them'. Do not give up on your story, be honest because no one can help you but yourself and that help starts with reaching out and accepting help from others to get you on track with fighting for yourself.

Resilience comes from adversity, in the words of Dr Anwar. Remember that breaking does not mean you cannot put yourself back together, my life has been in shards and I have managed to rebuild it time and time again, made peace with what I have done and what I have been through, who I have hurt and who I have made distrust me and I work to better myself and show I can be trusted.

Life is worth living, it might not seem like it at the moment, but I promise you, it is. You are one in a million, somehow at some point in time, God (or the universe etc) saw a need for you in this world. See years ago I would not think that at 23 years old I would still be alive, I honestly thought I would have died due to Ana or suicide and it was a harsh pill to swallow but I honestly thought that was where my life was heading. Now look at me, look at my journey, what I have achieved through it all, I survived.

So, my overall advice is to keep fighting and do not let your illness win because it is possible to survive this and it is possible through the pain of recovery to build yourself a better life. Remember recovery is not linear and falling down does not mean the fight is over, you can win as long as you are not looking backwards. I did a scrapbook this year of all of my photos from bodychecks and life in general where I have been sick, this way in a very perverse way, I have something to show for all those years of suffering and I can shut it away without losing a big part of my life.

In another sick way, my anorexic brain is proud of those images, but I know that the images now serve as a warning to me to never go back. All I can see is pain in those images now. At the start of writing this book I was beating myself up about the fact that I had relapsed but, now I have nothing but admiration for myself and my resilience so yeah... I will blow my own trumpet here because I won.

Do not give in or believe you are worthless, you can fight this, I did not think I would make it to 2021 and now just a few days away I sit with a full tummy sipping on a cup of tea finishing my story with Ana. My story will probably continue with her in the background, but that is ok because we all have parts of ourselves, we do not like and for me that part is her.

See...
In the field where the sunflowers grow you can find this woman with her face forever towards the sun.

'Turn your face towards the sun and the shadows will fall behind you.'

With thanks to my family, friends, and medical team. Acknowledgements:
Helen Shelton
Joshua Gibson
Phil Shelton
Danielle Rudkin
Dean Rudkin
Wednesday Stretton
Dr Adcock
Dr Anwar
Julie
Kev Wise

Printed in Great Britain
by Amazon